I have never read such a vivid account of what it is like to have grown up during the Cultural Revolution in China, especially for a young artist. The story is made all the more tangible by the constant references to food.

I have heard Guo Yue play his music, I have eaten his food, and can guarantee he delivers in a magical way.

What he and Clare have created with this book will leave no one wanting, and everyone hungry.

Peter Gabriel

Reading this book, I could taste the love in Chinese melody and hear the music in Chinese taste.

Xinran

Thank goodness Xiao Yue was listening when Hu Hai Chan said 'If you work hard on your music ... you will have good food'. Through Guo Yue's touching account of his childhood and love of food and music, you learn everything you need to know about family life in China during the Cultural Revolution. The story is told with a modesty and simple truth that is typical of the man himself – one of the greatest flute players in the world.

George Fenton, award-winning film, theatre and
television composer

A great story. A great man. A great cook.

Helen Baxendale

*Yue's cooking is like his music: fresh, delightful and unexpected ...
Along with our students, I have been eagerly awaiting this fascinating
book, where food, history and music combine to create a feast for the
senses.*

Camilla Schneideman, Divertimenti Cookery School,
London

Music, Food and Love

A Memoir

.

GUO YUE

AND CLARE FARROW

PORTRAIT

Visit the Portrait website!

PORTRAIT Piatkus publishes a wide range of non-fiction, including biography, history, science, music, popular culture and sport.

If you want to:
- read descriptions of our popular titles
- buy our books over the Internet
- take advantage of our special offers
- enter our monthly competition
- learn more about your favourite Piatkus authors

VISIT OUR WEBSITE AT: www.portraitbooks.co.uk

First published in Great Britain in 2005 by **Portrait**, an imprint of
Piatkus Books Ltd
5 Windmill Street,
London WIT 2JA
email: info@piatkus.co.uk

ISBN 0 7499 5078 1

Illustrations by Qu Lei Lei
Text design by Paul Saunders
Edited by Anthea Matthison and Penny Phillips

This book has been printed on paper manufactured
with respect for the environment using wood from
managed sustainable resources

Typeset by Phoenix Photosetting, Chatham, Kent
Printed and bound in Great Britain by
Mackays of Chatham, Chatham, Kent

Dedicated to the memory of my mother,
Zhao Su Lin, who loved poetry, nature, music and food

And to my children, Ying-Ying (Music Music),
Lu-Duo (Many Ways), Bei-Sheng (Sound of the North)
and Lan-Tien (Blue Sky)

The Natural Mode

from *The Twenty-four Modes of Poetry,* by the
Tang Dynasty poet SIKONG TU (837–908)

Choose plain words
To voice simple thoughts
As if, meeting suddenly with a recluse,
You have a revelation of the Truth.
Beside the winding brook,
In the green shade of pines,
One man is gathering firewood,
Another is playing the lute ...
Follow your natural bent
And wonders come unsought;
So, at a chance encounter
You hear rare music!

(from *Poetry and Prose of the Tang and Song,*
translated by Yang Xianyi and Gladys Yang, Chinese
Literature Press, Beijing, and Panda Books, 1984,
copyright Foreign Languages Press, Beijing, China)

CONTENTS

·

Acknowledgements

The stories and images of my childhood in *Music, Food and Love* have come from my own memories and perceptions. I apologise for any unintended errors of fact. Each individual experiences life in a unique way and, even side by side, two people will have a different story to tell. This is mine. To begin, I would like to thank my wife Clare for writing this book with me. Without her constant belief, understanding and creativity, it would not have been possible: she has given me a voice on paper. Together, we would like to thank our agent Laetitia Rutherford, of Toby Eady Associates, whose vision and encouragement have been instrumental in bringing this book to life; it has been a great pleasure to work with her. We would also like to thank everyone at Piatkus Books for their enthusiasm and sensitivity in handling the manuscript: in particular Judy Piatkus, our wonderful editors Gill Bailey and Jo Brooks, Anthea Matthison for her thorough reading of the text, Philip Cotterell and Jana Sommerlad. We are delighted to be including illustrations by our friend Qu Lei-Lei, to accompany the memoir, and thank this talented artist for contributing so beautifully to our book. We are also grateful to Wu Chengdong, of the Foreign Languages Press in Beijing, for giving us his kind permission to publish the lines of Tang dynasty poetry. And to the following, for their encouragement and support, we give our heartfelt thanks: Liu Qing Puo, whose memories of my very early childhood have been invaluable; the Guo family; Camilla Schneidemann of the Divertimenti Cookery School in London; Lesley and Tony Farrow; and our very special Ying-Ying, Lu-Duo, Bei-Sheng and Lan-Tien.

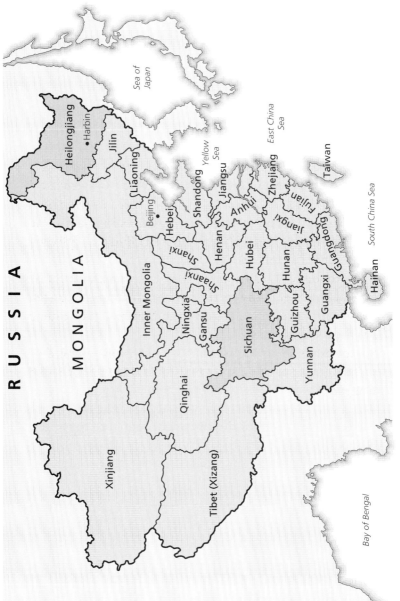

Map of China

Notes on pronunciation

When you read this book, I would like you to experience something of the Mandarin language, which is so musical with its four different tones. To do so, you need to remember that the following letters or groups of letters in pin-yin, the method for transcribing Chinese into the English alphabet, are pronounced as follows:

x is pronounced as *sh*; an as *en*; zh as *j*; q as *ch*; e (for example, in my name, Yue) as the e sounds in *er*; z as *ds*; c as *ts*; u as *oo*; o as *or*; ui as *way*; ou as ow sounds in *bowl* and i after z or s as the e sounds in *er*.

So, for example, my sister Xuan's name is pronounced as *shuen*; xiao (little) as *shiao*; si (silk) as *ser* and my family name Guo as *guor*.

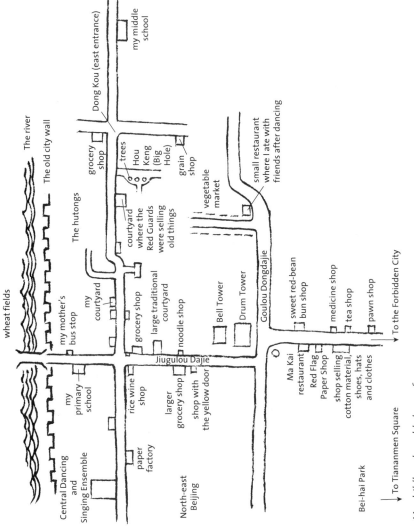

The river

The old city wall

wheat fields

The hutongs

Dong Kou (east entrance)

my middle school

grocery shop

trees

Hou Keng (Big Hole)

grain shop

courtyard where the Red Guards were selling old things

vegetable market

small restaurant where I ate with friends after dancing

my mother's bus stop

my courtyard

grocery shop

large traditional courtyard

Bell Tower

Drum Tower

Goulou Dongdajie

sweet red-bean bun shop

medicine shop

tea shop

pawn shop

To the Forbidden City

my primary school

rice wine shop

larger grocery shop

shop with the yellow door

noodle shop

Jiugulou Dajie

Ma Kai restaurant

Red Flag Paper Shop

shop selling cotton material, shoes, hats and clothes

Central Dancing and Singing Ensemble

paper factory

North-east Beijing

Bei-hai Park

To Tiananmen Square

My childhood world, drawn from memory

A note on the recipes

We would like you to consider the recipes in this book as belonging to the memoir, as being part of the reading experience, as well as enabling you to recreate the sights, sounds and tastes of my childhood through your own cooking. For this reason, we have often referred you to specific recipes at the end of a chapter: dishes that are either mentioned by name in the text or illustrate that part of the memoir. The rhythms, actions, colours and ingredients that are described in the recipes themselves will enhance your understanding of the story, so please feel free to turn to those pages as you read *Music, Food and Love*. Some of the most symbolic dishes, the handmade noodles and dumplings, for example, are complex recipes involving a sequence of repetitive, ritual-like movements and techniques that require much practice. In this sense, traditional Chinese cooking can be likened to the Chinese arts of music and brush painting. These recipes are challenging to learn on paper, but we have included them in this book because the time, skill, repetition and meaning involved lie at the very heart of Chinese home cooking and were the foundations of my childhood experience.

Part One

·

A MEMOIR

INTRODUCTION

I am a musician, a Chinese bamboo flutes player and composer, not a professional cook. But I have had a passion for cooking since my childhood in Beijing and for me, music and food have always been equally important. I believe both are essential to life. Both are creative and give pleasure. In this book I want to give you a taste of Chinese home cooking – traditional recipes passed on in families and among friends, based on a few, simple ingredients, a natural approach to taste, colour and texture, and an innate love of good food.

This book is also the story of my childhood in a musical family, before, during and after the Cultural Revolution, a time in which music and cooking were the only constant forms of education I received. I learned my cooking the traditional way, through watching and imitating my sisters and the traditional musicians who lived in our courtyard. Through experience, I discovered the right timing to achieve the most vibrant colours, the lightness of touch and intensity of heat required to combine many ingredients into a harmony of tastes, and the right smell in the wind, which means something delicious is about to be served. Just as I learned to play the bamboo flutes by observing, listening and repeating, practising until I knew the notes and rhythms off by heart and could then put my own feeling and spirit into the music; so with cooking I studied through my senses, until I had the freedom to be creative in my own right.

In recreating these dishes in your own kitchens, I hope that the sounds, rhythms, tastes and colours that you encounter will bring the images of my childhood closer to your imagination.

Chapter 1

COOKING IN MY CHILDHOOD

When I was a child in the 1960s, growing up in the over-crowded *hutongs*, the maze of alleys and courtyards in the north-east of Beijing, people would always greet their friends and neighbours with the words '*Che fan le ma?*' (Have you eaten?). If the answer was yes, then they would immediately ask, '*Che de she ma?*' (What did you eat?) and expect a detailed, colourful description. From the beginning of the Cultural Revolution in the summer of 1966, people were not free to express their thoughts about so many things – books, poetry, music, society, even love, anything that was not precisely in tune with the Revolution. But with cooking, though ingredients were limited, people were still free to discuss their ideas, to share thoughts and opinions about food, to argue passionately as the Chinese love to do. Food and nature were the two most frequent subjects of private conversation: the colours of a bird and the pattern of its song, or the beauty of a tree in blossom, the texture of a veg-etable dish or the intricate folds of a handmade dumpling, these were subjects that were not officially controlled by

5

anyone. People were free to let their words and imaginations take flight.

My family lived in two rooms, in the corner of a courtyard which had once been part of a temple dating back to the Ming Dynasty. The old wooden gate from the alley into the courtyard was part of the original building – I remember there were wild flowers growing on the top of this gate – but the rest of the courtyard had been rebuilt in the 1930s. My father, a Chinese *erhu* (two-stringed violin) soloist, belonged to the Central Dancing and Singing Ensemble in Beijing, a prestigious company controlled by the government and employing around 300 musicians, singers and dancers. These artists and their

The Guo family, before I was born: (from left to right, back row) a cousin, my mother Zhao Su Lin and my father Guo Zhen Dong; (middle row) my sisters Yan, Xuan and Kai; (front row) my brother Yi and sister Liang

families were housed together in a large compound, not far from the beautiful Bell Tower (Zhonglou) and Drum Tower (Goulou), both dating from 1420 during the Ming Dynasty.

My father, who was from the Henan Province in the north of China, had studied his musical instrument in a conservatoire and had taught music in the Sichuan Province, where he had met my mother; but such an educated background was not in tune with the communist thinking of Mao Zedong. Audition groups were sent by the government into the countryside, to find the best traditional musicians, dancers and singers, many of whom could not read or even write their own names, and had only ever performed at village festivals, weddings and funerals. These artists were introduced into my father's company as 'treasures from the countryside': they couldn't read or write musical notation but they had a special quality, an individuality that set them apart from conservatoire-trained musicians like my father. There was something wild and free about them and they performed traditional tunes and love songs with a kind of raw passion that fascinated me as a child. The most talented were given high salaries and opportunities in conducting and composing that would have been unthinkable before the emergence of communism in China.

String players were allocated rooms for their families in the main artists' compound which had been built after Mao's Liberation of China in 1949, when he founded the People's Republic. In the same street, there were many traditional courtyards, a primary school and two small factories – one making paper, the other soy sauce. The big wooden gate of this large, modern compound opened into a courtyard garden which flowered with cherry blossom in the spring, and there were stages and practice rooms, where my sisters loved to watch the dancers rehearsing their performances. But the gate was closed at ten o'clock every evening and my father was not free to come and go as he wished; he felt there were people watching him. And so, before I was born, my family made a special request to live outside the main compound, in one of the nearby *hutongs* (traditional alleys).

My sisters remember how happy my father was, on moving to Yu Huang Ge Hutong (jade emperor temple alley), where workers at the imperial court were said to have lived during the Ming Dynasty. Our courtyard housed five families of musicians, mostly from the countryside, who played traditional Chinese wind instruments; but in our neighbouring courtyard there was also a doctor living with his family in the alley and there were people practising many other professions. My father loved the fact that we were close enough to the government grocery shop to hear people shout, 'Tomatoes have arrived today!' and my sisters could be first in the queue. Also he was free to walk by himself in the evenings, whenever he liked, and to go to a little traditional wine shop where he could buy his strong rice wine. Just standing outside, I remember, you could already smell the powerful contents of this shop. Inside there was only earth on the ground. The wine was kept in a big clay pot, with a heavy wooden lid wrapped in a dirty-looking cloth. The shopkeeper would use a small bamboo pot on a long stick to take out a measure of the rice wine and pour it into a glass bottle using a little funnel. My father would take his own bottle each time, to be refilled with the cheapest rice wine.

Following the arrival of these traditional singers, dancers and musicians from the countryside, my mother was given the task of teaching the women singers to read and write. They respected, and grew to love my mother, whom they called Zhao Lao-shi (old master Zhao, her family name), often coming to her with their personal problems. These young singers missed their families, the traditions and nature they had left behind. Some had come from the northern part of China known as Yellow Earth, outside Yan'an in the Shaanxi Province, which had become the communist base for Mao's

Red Army during his fighting with the Guomindang: he had wanted to honour this region of China. Often they felt guilty for leaving their parents in the countryside, while they were singing and dancing, and many experienced relationship problems inside the gates of the compound. As artists from the countryside, they were given extra ration tickets for rice, the most highly prized grain in Beijing, but all they really wanted was flour, to make dumplings, pancakes and especially noodles, the traditional food of the poor, dry Yellow Earth, where wheat, not rice, is grown. When they came to our home in the alley, they felt freer and more individual: there was a sense of intimacy as you walked through the wooden gate into our small, traditional courtyard, so different from the artists' compound. The women loved to talk to my mother about their families and to make noodles by hand. Their favourite dish was a large bowl of fresh noodle soup with carrot, *bai-cai* (Chinese leaf) and chilli, accompanied by a raw *da cong* (a big white onion, much hotter than a spring onion): holding it in one hand, with a pair of chopsticks in the other, they would eat the noodles and onion together, drinking the soup directly from the bowl. This was like heaven, they said! Afterwards they would sing for my mother, with voices that sounded like the mountains: completely natural, beautiful and untrained.

Music and food existed side by side in our courtyard, where the sounds of musicians practising their instruments and singing were regularly accompanied by the rhythmic chopping, dramatic sounds and irresistible smells of Chinese home cooking. When my parents first moved to the alley, they bought a wooden bed and a round wooden table, painted yellow, which we used for eating, writing, chopping vegetables, whatever we were doing: it was the centre of our family life. The frame of the wooden bed had two shapes cut out of it for decoration, one at either end: two spiralling treble clef signs from Western musical notation, so different to Chinese notation, which consists of numbers and short lines. As a very small child, I used to like standing at the end of my parents' bed, tracing the continuous line of the treble clef with my finger; its curling form suggested another world to me and, looking back, it now seems an appropriate image for the beginning of my childhood story, in which music and the simple routines of everyday life are so closely entwined.

RECIPES

- Handmade flour noodles *see pages* 244–5
- *Tang mian* (Noodle soup) with tomato and carrot *see pages* 245–7

Chapter 2

A SLICE OF APPLE

I was given the name Yue (Leap Forward) because I was born in 1958, the year of the Great Leap Forward (Da Yue Jin). In my family there is a mixture of artistic and revolutionary names. My brother is called Yi (meaning Art), my first sister is called Kai (Victory), my third sister Yan (meaning Swallow, a bird that my mother loved); but as a child I was always proud to have a name that represented revolution. Many of my contemporaries had been given the same name, so if you walked into my classroom at school and called out 'Yue!', half the boys would turn around. But apart from my mother and father, who called me Xiao Yue (Little Leap Forward), I was always known as Guo Yue, Guo (Kingdom) being my family name.

Mao's Great Leap Forward policy of 1958 was an attempt to revolutionise agriculture and the steel industry in one sudden, experimental step, creating people's communes that led to chaos in the countryside and a famine that took millions of lives. Outside the cities, people had been forced to hand over their woks and cooking utensils, which were melted down in a hopeless attempt to create large quantities of steel. In Beijing, people were told that the famine had been caused by a series of natural disasters: too much rain had resulted in flooding, which had destroyed the crops. There were too many people and not enough food in the cities, so ingredients were highly rationed, especially wheat flour and rice, the best, most delicious food in China. The rice fields, people were told, had been particularly affected.

Everyone in Beijing was given a book of ration tickets, to purchase 24 *jin* (1 *jin* is a little over 450 g, or 1lb) of grain each month (the rations were much less for a child). This worked out as 7 *jin* of white rice, 7 *jin* of white wheat flour and 10 *jin* of yellow corn flour made from maize, which is low in nutrition and quite rough, but can be made into a kind of corn bread, porridge or *bian*, a thick pancake. As a baby I was given a lot of the yellow corn porridge which we call *zhou*, similar to Italian polenta. I was never breastfed, because my mother returned to work soon after I was born. Instead, the government provided ration tickets for babies in Beijing to be given small quantities of cow's milk, which had to be boiled because it was unpasteurised. The only other nutrition that was readily available was *bai-cai* in the winter, with tomatoes and carrots in the summer. There were ration tickets for other essential ingredients, including cooking oil, sugar, eggs and pork, but even with these my family remembers that certain foods were very difficult to find. Each adult was supposed to be able to purchase four eggs a month, half a *jin* of pork and a little packet of sugar. But even if you joined the long queues outside the government shops, you might only be able to get the equivalent of 60 g (2 oz) of meat, if any at all, and perhaps the same amount of sugar. Fresh eggs were extremely hard to come by. The amount of grain allocated to each person, however, varied according to their work: metalworkers in the factories were given extra rations, around 30 *jin* of grain, though this was less for women doing exactly the same job;

teachers were given 29 *jin*, and musicians like my father were given 28 *jin* of grain.

White wheat flour became something precious in our family and only once or twice a month would my sisters use our rations to make the light, hot steamed buns that we call *man-tou*. From an early age, my youngest sister Liang was given the task of carefully measuring out the quantity of white flour, using a ruler to smooth what remained. Sometimes, she remembers, when no one was looking, she would add just a little bit more. To make a dough that would rise, my sisters used what is known as the 'mother yeast': a piece of dough that has been kept out for a few days near the hot stove, so that it goes sour and changes texture. This mother yeast was often shared between neighbours in the alleys. My sisters would then add this to a fresh, new dough made from flour and water, leaving it under a warm jacket or blanket for a couple of days. The mother yeast would make the dough rise, but it would be sour. So my sisters would dissolve a little white cube (*jian*, a substance from the earth, they said) in some hot water, adding the resulting yellow liquid to the dough a little at a time and kneading it constantly, until the dough no longer smelt sour and was ready to be formed into *man-tou*.

My mother used to tell me how I would sit on her wooden bed when I was eight or nine months old, watching my sisters kneading the dough, my arms moving up and down in excitement. My sisters would form the dough into little domes, curved on the top, flat on the bottom. When these emerged from the bamboo steamer, they would be twice the size. In normal circumstances, in a family of eight as we were, each person would have two or three *man-tou*, to accompany a number of dishes, including meat and eggs. But at that time, we would each have only one, or sometimes even less, with a simple dish of *bai-cai* cooked with a little finely chopped spring onion and soy sauce. To 'fill the gap' afterwards, as the Chinese say, we would then have to eat the yellow corn porridge, served with pickled vegetables from the carrot family. My mother always said how moved she was, watching my pale face as I was happily eating my steamed *man-tou* and then seeing me cry as my sisters gave me the corn porridge. Now as a musician, when I perform in Italy, though I adore Italian food, I have to explain to my hosts why it is that I can never eat polenta.

During the day, while my mother was teaching, I was looked after by an old woman from the countryside with tiny bound feet, whom I called 'Lao-Lao' (the word for grand-mother). She was living with her son who was working in a factory in Beijing and she looked after me in her courtyard every day from morning until evening. I remember she was a beautiful old woman, with silver hair drawn back into a bun which she covered with a black net. She was very thin, but strong, and always wore traditional blue clothes, with buttons down one side. My memories of her are like distant shadows, but I know that she had a nice temper and used to sing tradi-tional songs to me from the countryside. My sisters remember how she would sometimes make *Ge de tang* (flour-lump soup), which I loved. Using very hot oil, she would fry a little finely chopped spring onion, adding a few drops of soy sauce and some cold water, followed by one or two drops of sesame seed oil. This created the basic taste, with the only ingredients that were available to her. When the water was boiling, she would add a few drops to a tiny amount of white flour, mixing it into little pieces with a pair of chopsticks. These lumps of flour were then added to the soup. The con-trast between this soup, with its precious tastes of flour, spring onion, soy sauce and sesame seed oil, and the bland-ness of the yellow corn porridge must have impressed me, even as a small child.

I was three years old when I began attending a nursery school, called Wen Hua Bu, run by the Culture Department of Beijing. It was in a beautiful courtyard. The large rooms had high wooden ceilings, stone floors and grey tiles on the roofs. My sisters, especially Yan, would take me early in the morning and collect me in the evening, so I would eat in the nursery with the other children. By 1961, a more rational approach to agriculture was bringing the famine in the countryside to an end, and food rations in Beijing were beginning to improve: gradually there would be more fresh, seasonal vegetables, even some fruit, and a little more meat available in the shops, though this was still highly rationed.

In my nursery we were given noodle soup or fried noodles in the middle of the day, with *bai-cai* in the winter, tomatoes, carrots, spinach and different kinds of beans in the summer. I was not familiar with fruit at all, and my lasting memory of

My family, after my father's death: (from left to right, back row) Xuan, Kai, my mother, her niece, my sister Yan; (front row) Liang, myself and Yi

being at nursery is sitting on a little wooden chair, watching the teacher cutting up a fresh apple into many slices, shaped like a half-moon. I would be given one slice of apple which I would eat at great speed. But there was never enough, I always wanted more, and the taste of that apple would stay in my mind for a long time afterwards.

Chapter 3

WHITE SWANS

My mother was a romantic figure to me. Born in 1917, in the year of the Dragon, she had grown up as the daughter of a wealthy lawyer in the city of Harbin, in the northernmost province of China, which is part of Manchuria, on the border with Russia. When she was a little girl, her family had had many servants and cooks, who prepared feasts of colourful dishes that filled my imagination. One of the most traditional dishes in Harbin, and my mother's favourite, was *hong shao rou* (red stewed pork), which is cooked for a long time with potatoes, dried mushrooms, star anise and *fen-tiao*, which are long brownish-coloured 'ribbons' (similar in shape to Italian tagliatelle), made from beans or sweet potato. Later on in her life, when we were living in the Beijing alleys and pork was highly rationed, if one of my sisters was invited to a friend's courtyard, or to the Central Dancing and Singing Ensemble, to eat *hong shao rou*, they would always bring a little home for my mother, knowing how much she adored it. She didn't mind how late it was; she would sit up in bed, happily eating and telling us stories about her childhood.

Her father had had an arranged marriage with a girl from the countryside, who had tiny bound feet. But my mother was a modern girl, whose feet were never bound, and who lived as a child with the influences of Russia all around her. After the October Revolution of 1917, many Russian aristocrats and others who opposed the Bolsheviks fled across the border into China. They settled in Harbin, already a city under Russian influence after the construction of the Chinese Eastern Railway in the late nineteenth century, which provided a route for Russians to travel through Manchuria to Vladivostok. In my mother's childhood, the Chinese called Russia by its old name, E Guo, and they called these Russian émigrés Bai E (White Russians). Harbin became a centre for old Russian culture, a stunning city which featured many Russian churches and houses. But when I was little I couldn't understand what my mother meant by Bai E: in Chinese, 'e' also means 'swan', so whenever she talked about these romantic, foreign people who had fled their country, I always had an image of white swans in my mind.

My mother loved everything Russian: the language, which she spoke fluently (as well as English, which she studied at school), Russian clothes, literature, poetry and architecture. Her best friend had been a Russian girl who wore a white fur coat in the winter, just like the heroine of Tolstoy's *War and Peace*, and my mother's favourite novel, *Anna Karenina*, books that we would only be able to read in secret. My mother thought that Russian girls were very striking, with their different-coloured eyes and hair, which was sometimes really golden. And she would tell us how beautiful she too had been in those days. Sometimes her father would take her, in his horse and trap, into the centre of Harbin, to go to the theatre or to see a film in the cinema, or to go shopping for clothes. Most of all she remembered his long, elegant white gloves, as he held the reins of his horse. In the winter she would go ice-skating, wearing colourful skirts and fur coats: it was the place to meet, to be seen and to fall in love.

Very rarely did she speak about the Japanese occupation of Manchuria, which had resulted in her learning to speak Japanese. I remember only one such story. My mother was travelling on a train in Manchuria, when it was stopped by Japanese soldiers who wanted to search all the passengers. She had to lift her heavy trunk down and open it. A Japanese soldier then lifted out her clothes and belongings, including her fur coat, one by one, using the point of his bayonet. Much later in her life, when she was living in our courtyard, she would see Pu Yi, the last emperor of the Qing Dynasty, the 'puppet emperor' in Manchuria under the Japanese, as an old man, sweeping a street near Jingshan Gongyuan (Park of the Beautiful View), a short distance from the Forbidden City (Gugong) where he had become emperor in 1908, at the age of three. My mother explained that he was living in a courtyard close by, working mostly as a gardener. 'I felt sorry for him, Xiao Yue,' she said.

My favourite stories, though, were always about food. She would tell us how the peasants in the countryside outside Harbin would make *jiaozi* (traditional dumplings) at Chinese New Year or, as we say, Chun Jie (Spring Festival) in late January or early February. They would make thousands of dumplings filled with *bai-cai* or *suan-cai* (preserved cabbage) and some with meat, enough to last right through to April. The earth was so frozen at that time of year, they couldn't plough or work the land at all, so they would line big clay pots (originally used for water) with layer upon layer of dumplings and store them outside. Frozen in this way, the dumplings kept their shape and intricate folds beautifully. Every day they would go out to collect the dumplings, which were delicious when boiled. So for those few, freezing months they just slept and ate good food. I loved that story very much!

My mother liked beautiful things: the poetry of old China, the style of the Qing Dynasty; she loved colourful, fashionable clothes, books, and make-up, all things that would be declared *petit bourgeois* in the Cultural Revolution.

One of the few things she still kept from her childhood, until the beginning of the Revolution in 1966, was a Russian clock which was pale green and gold, with crystal decoration and a round, clear face. It was shaped like a Russian church. I found myself irresistibly drawn to it because, through the crystal, you could see some of the parts moving. One day, when I was five years old, I was overcome with curiosity to see all the inner workings of my mother's clock. I started to take out one screw, and then the other one became loose, and then the middle part came out, and then the back of the clock itself, until I could see so many moving parts, it was fascinating. But afterwards, it was impossible for anyone to work out how to put all the parts back together, and the clock never worked again. I still remember the excitement I felt that day, and the fact that neither my mother, nor my sisters, were angry with me. I think my mother believed in curiosity, that it was part of being creative.

Chapter 4

MUSIC IN MY COURTYARD

When I think of my father, Guo Zhen Dong (his name meant 'shaking the East'), it is his instrument that I remember most of all. The *erhu* is the traditional Chinese violin, originally from Mongolia. My father's instrument was an old one, made from a dark reddish wood, very smooth, with a *long tou*, a dragon's head, carved on the top. The *erhu* has only two metal strings, and the bow, made from a wood that can bend like willow, with the hairs of a horse's tail, is positioned in-between the strings: unlike the bow of a Western violin, it cannot be separated from the instrument. The sound box is shaped like a hexagon, covered by a layer of snakeskin to create the unique, often sad sound. The movement of the bow between the two strings is restricted but, within these simple boundaries and with highly skilled fingers, the *erhu* can produce the most extraordinary, poetic music. It is famous in traditional Chinese music for imitating the neighing and galloping of wild horses across the open plains of Mongolia. But it is also used in old classical melodies about nature: sad, poetic tunes about the moon or the lakes

and mountains of China's vast landscape. What I loved the most about my father's *erhu* was the case. It was a black wooden case with a red velvet lining and inside there were a number of compartments: one for the piece of wax, which he used to prepare the strings of the bow; another for a packet of new strings, in case one broke; and one long compartment for pencils to mark his music. This was the one I loved, because sometimes he would hide little presents inside for me.

One evening, when I was four or five years old, I was inside our home when I heard my father returning from the theatre where he had just been performing with the Dancing and Singing Ensemble. 'Xiao Yue,' he called, 'come into the court-yard.' It was getting dark outside and when I was little I was afraid of the dark, especially in the alleys beyond our home. But then I heard my father playing the first few bars of a tra-ditional tune on his *erhu* and I ventured out, towards his music. 'Look, Xiao Yue,' he said, showing me his empty hands and empty instrument case. Seeing my disappointment, he said, 'Wait, let me do some magic for you.' With a theatrical movement of his hands, he made a pinky-red boiled sweet appear out of his instrument case. I can still remember the exact taste of that sweet, which I loved because it had travelled all the way home from the theatre in the long compartment of his case, next to his dark red violin.

After a performance, in which he would play traditional tunes which had often been given new words, the musicians would sometimes be rewarded with presents of food: a fresh apple, two bananas or a sweet red-bean bun. My father would bring these home and cut them into many pieces, giving them to my mother and to all of us, but never eating any himself.

There were no singers in our courtyard; they were all instrumental players, although my father had a fine tenor voice and conducted the choir in the Dancing and Singing Ensemble. Out of the five traditional musicians in our court-yard, my father was the only string player and the only

My father, Guo Zhen Dong

performer who had been trained in a conservatoire. All the other musicians played wind instruments from the countryside, which is why I think they had all been housed outside the Dancing and Singing Ensemble compound: their instruments were so loud that it was difficult for a string player to concentrate when they were all practising! Normally, string players didn't mix with wind players but my sisters remember my father enjoying their company. Before he became ill, my father was full of imagination and fun: he loved life, eating and drinking, singing and telling jokes. And on first moving into the alley, my family would often eat with the other musicians and their children, outside in the courtyard. They would set up two wooden trestles with one long piece of wood, and everyone would cook something to share, putting all the different dishes together. It was very spontaneous.

After his death in 1964, my sisters would tell me how creative my father had been with his cooking: 'Yue, you are just like our father. With only a few ingredients you are like a little bird, you are so happy that you sing, and you can still be creative with only two potatoes, a carrot and a little cucumber. Like him, you can make so many dishes.'

Chapter 5

BAI MIAN SHU SHENG (WHITE FLOUR BOOK BOY)

'Xiao Yue,' my father said to me when I was four or five years old, 'you have *zui yan* (drunkard eyes).' In Chinese, this has a beautiful, dreamy, artistic meaning. My eyes are a very light brown in comparison to most Chinese eyes, my hair is not so black, and I had an unusually pale face as a child. Friends would say, 'Guo Yue doesn't look like the rest of the family,' and my mother would laugh: 'Perhaps he's Russian, and not my child at all!'

Friends in the alleys would sometimes bring me a few baby silkworms as a present. They would arrive in a little box, with some special leaves from a tree that bore fruit similar to raspberries. I know now that this must have been a mulberry tree. As far as I knew then, these were the only leaves that the silkworms could eat, so I would go to the Dancing and Singing Ensemble, through the big wooden gates and into the courtyard where one of these special trees was growing, and I would climb up to collect a handful of leaves. But you had to be careful climbing this tree because there were caterpillars on the bark that had a lot of spikes on their patterned bodies and, if you weren't careful, they would take the skin off your legs. But once I had collected some leaves, it was a fantastic feeling. I would take them back to my courtyard and wipe the dust off with a cloth. The leaves were so fresh and green, I wouldn't have minded eating them myself! The baby silk-worms were only about 1 cm long and very thin but I would keep on feeding them with leaves until they were 4–5 cm long and fat, with white bodies and dark brown heads. I remember them having lots of little legs, which would stick on to the leaves when I tried to pull them off. I used to put them on the big circular straw mat that my sisters used for arranging dumplings and watch them eating their leaves.

Once they were fully grown, they could start to give silk. Using a white porcelain rice bowl, I would put a sheet of white writing paper over the top of the bowl, fastening it with a rubber band. Then I placed a few of the silkworms on to the paper and they would start to make silk, moving their heads as they worked. I loved the fact that they laboured all through the night, without any sleep. After one or two nights, I forget how long, the silkworms had made a smooth, circular piece of yellow, shiny silk, right up to the edge of the paper. I watched them all the time, thinking that the silkworm was one of the best creatures in the world. My mother told me that when they had made all the silk that they could, they would cease to exist inside their cocoons.

In China, we call the silkworm inside the cocoon *jin-gang* (gold metal). The cocoon itself is pale brown in colour, but if you open it up, which I did out of curiosity, the silkworm has turned into a dark brown, shiny spiral. If you hold it, the pointed bit at the top of the spiral spins. My friend Xiao-Xiao's father used to cook these *jin-gang*, frying them until they were crispy and then dipping them into a sauce. I could never forgive him for doing this. If you left the cocoon alone, a large brown silk moth would emerge and fly across the room to the white net curtains at our window, which had turned grey with the dust from the alleys. I used to catch the silk moth in my hands and take it outside, releasing it in the courtyard.

The piece of yellow silk I would take down from the paper and cut into a square shape. I just liked to look at it. I remember wanting to bond with the silkworms. They seemed more intelligent than humans and they always smelled of the fresh green leaves. If I think about it, I can still smell those leaves.

At that time in Beijing, near the Bell and Drum Towers, there were still many small, traditional shops, selling handmade noodles, different kinds of tea, sweet red-bean buns and herbal medicines. Among them was a traditional pawn shop called Wei Tuo Hang, meaning 'I ask you to do this for me', where you could take things you wanted to sell. There were many big steps up to the door and inside there was a tall wooden desk, so high that a child couldn't see what was on top of it.

After my father's death in 1964, when my family was no longer receiving a musician's salary from the Dancing and Singing Ensemble, we were very poor. My mother began to borrow money from her friends and school, ten *yuan* at a time, until she found that she had already borrowed and spent her next month's salary: she had no money left to buy food. One day, when there were just the two of us at home, I kept telling my mother that I was hungry, but there was no grain to eat. Then I saw her going into our *li wu* (inner room) where my sisters slept and where we kept our special things. She opened a wooden case and got out my father's dark blue performance clothes. '*Zou-ba* (let's go),' she said. She took my hand, and we walked together through the alleys and streets to Wei Tuo Hang. I remember feeling her sadness but only half understanding: 'But we can get them back again, can't we, Ma? I want to have Ba-Ba's music clothes.' My mother kept saying, 'Yes, yes.' My father's blue woollen performance jacket and long traditional *chang-shan* were placed on the high wooden desk, and my mother sold them for four *yuan* and five *mao qian*, enough to buy some essential grain and vegetables. (There are ten *mao* in one *yuan*, and at that time one *jin* of rice cost two *mao*.) 'Can we come back soon, Ma, to get them?' I asked. My mother said yes, although she must have known that they would be sold before we could have enough money to buy them back. My father's performance clothes, the only belongings he seemed to have apart from his traditional violin and instrument case, were very beautiful, but would have been sold cheaply at that time.

I held on to her hand as we walked towards the Drum Tower again and stopped outside a famous restaurant called Ma Kai (Horse Victory). I could see the steam coming out of the door as people were leaving and I could smell the *dou-fu* (fresh bean curd), meat and vegetables cooking. My mother looked at me. 'Xiao Yue, are you very hungry?' she asked. 'You know we have to buy rice and flour; but let's give ourselves a treat.' There were a lot of people in the restaurant that day, people with better salaries and fewer children, who were ordering *dou-fu*, beansprouts, red stewed pork and fish. We sat down together at a little wooden table and my mother ordered two bowls of plain rice. 'What dishes can we have, Ma?' I wanted to know. 'We will order one *hun-tun tang* (little dumpling soup) to have with our rice,' my mother replied, taking out *yi mao liu fen qian* (one *mao* and six *fen*: there are ten *fen* in one *mao*) from her purse. There were six little minced pork and ginger dumplings in the bowl of soup, which had been made from a stock comprising fish and meat bones, and any other leftovers that had been boiled overnight, so it was very nutritious. We had half each and poured it on to our rice. I poured a little soy sauce on to mine, and it was so delicious. In the restaurant that day they were also serving *chao san si* (fried three silk, a traditional name which refers to the preparation of the dish, in which the vegetables are cut as fine as silk). I still remember the smell: really earthy vegetables,

*With my mother, and sister
Liang, after my father's
death*

potato, carrot, red and green pepper, quick-fried in oil with salt. But I knew it was too expensive for us to order. Still, I walked home to our courtyard feeling very happy and thinking that I had the best mother. It was the first time I ever went to a restaurant.

My mother no longer had anyone to look after me while she was teaching; and so, when I was six and a half, I began attending the *xiao xue* (little or primary school), six months before I was supposed to start. On my first day, the teacher took one look at my pale face and decided to call me *Bai mian shu sheng*. I thought he was saying 'white *flour* book boy', because to my mind I immediately thought of *mian* as 'flour'. Only now, writing this, do I realise that I misunderstood him, that *mian*, spoken in a different tone, means 'face'. He was not as poetic as I had thought and I still prefer my first translation.

My school was in a beautiful old temple courtyard, the buildings once used for people to pray in and burn incense, with washed-out grey tiles on the roofs and high ceilings inside the *da dian* (big room), supported by huge wooden beams. In the heat of the summer, our classroom was still cool inside; in the freezing winters we had a big coal stove which had two doors that opened and closed, controlling the passage of air and the heat of the fire. Pupils would take it in turns to go into school early in the morning to get the fire going, so that it would be warm enough for our lessons to begin.

There were 38 children in my class, 19 girls and 19 boys. We each had a wooden desk, with a lid that opened up so you could keep your pencils and other things inside, and a wooden chair. You had to sit very straight with your hands behind your back, if you weren't writing or asking a question: then you had to put your elbow on the middle of the desk with your hand pointing directly into the air, waiting for the teacher to call out your name. I liked to sit with my hands clasped behind my back like this: you couldn't fall asleep in that position and it gave you excellent posture! According to tradition, boys were not allowed to speak even one sentence to girls in the class. Still, I used to stretch out one foot under my desk, trying to touch the padded shoes of the girl sitting in front of me. She must have known what I was doing but she kept perfectly still and composed, her long black plaits tied beautifully with silk ribbons.

We wore the same clothes to school, girls and boys alike: blue cotton trousers, black cotton shoes, a white shirt and a red cotton scarf, knotted in the front. This was supposed to represent the corner of the Chinese flag, which we called *wu xing hong qi* (five star flag): it was a symbol of communism, an idea that came from Russia I think. But you could only wear this part of the uniform if your behaviour in class was

In my primary school uniform, aged 7

good. When a teacher came into the class, we had to stand and salute to Chairman Mao, with one hand at an angle just above our heads.

Every morning, the whole school would do exercises outside in the courtyard: military-style music would be played through big speakers while we marched, lifting our arms high in the air and touching our toes in unison. After our exercises, we would begin our studies: mathematics and calligraphy training. We each had to bring in our own ink stone and calligraphy brush, which we kept inside our desks. My mother bought these for me very cheaply in a special shop near my alley that sold writing paper, sewing needles, candles, pencils and brushes. This shop had a yellow painted door and was one of the few shops I went in as a child that didn't smell of food: I liked that.

On my first day at school, my mother said to the teacher, 'I have noticed that Xiao Yue uses his left hand to draw and to hold his chopsticks. I think he is naturally left-handed.' 'We will correct him,' the teacher said. I was not allowed to be left-handed. Holding the calligraphy brush in my right hand, with a very straight arm, I had to write one character over and over again. I loved the smell of the ink on the stone and the rice paper which was divided into squares, one for each character, but I was very bad at calligraphy, which we call *da zi*. I didn't have the patience for it: in one lesson of 45 minutes we were supposed to write only ten characters. But, more than that, I found it difficult to work with my right hand: I felt distanced from what I was doing. So sometimes, when the teacher turned his back on the class, I would quickly transfer my brush to my left hand and then my writing felt so beautiful and free. But as soon as the teacher turned his attention back to the pupils and our calligraphy, I would have to return the brush to my right hand. I remember sitting at my desk, watching the other children carefully writing their characters. I always felt different to them: they had all been born in the year of the Chicken.

Being younger, I had been born in the year of the Dog, the only one in my class.

We were given ten minutes in-between each lesson. During the winter, in that short interval, I loved to sit next to the big stove. Sometimes I would bring a small piece of *man-tou* in my pocket: if you put both sides on to the metal ring of the stove, it became hot and crispy. Other children sometimes even brought a *baozi* to heat up on the stove: a special round dumpling stuffed with cabbage, egg and ginger. But this was only between classes. At the end of the morning we went home for lunch, returning later for afternoon lessons.

At other times of the year, we would go outside in those ten minutes to play, girls and boys together. There was only earth on the ground, so we couldn't play ball games. Sometimes we joined in with the girls' skipping games, although they were always much better than us. But mostly, as soon as we heard the school bell marking the end of a lesson, we would run outside to play table tennis: whoever got there first would be guaranteed a game. There were two table-tennis tables in our school, both made from bricks with smooth cement on the top. Bricks also took the place of the net but these were quite adequate for our purposes. Boys had to bring in their own table-tennis bats and balls but my family couldn't afford to buy them, so I always had to borrow a bat from one of my friends. I loved playing table tennis and I remember asking my mother if she could buy me a bat. 'No, Xiao Yue, they are too expensive.' I was so upset and angry with her that I lay down outside in our courtyard to demonstrate, to make her buy a bat for me. I lay on the cold ground, my head on my hands, for five hours. But it was no use: my mother did not buy me a table-tennis bat.

RECIPES

- *Hun-tun tang* (little dumpling soup) *see pages* 236–8
- *Chao san si* (fried three silk) *see pages* 192–4

Chapter 6

SU LIN (CALMNESS OF THE FOREST)

My mother's first name was Su Lin, meaning 'calmness of the forest': I remember her telling me this. In Chinese, the word 'calmness' is composed of two characters: one meaning 'green' (in a deeper sense, 'nature'), the other 'struggle'. Together they mean 'calmness' because in Chinese philosophy nature has to fight, to struggle, in order to attain stillness and harmony. It is a poetic name and fitting for my mother who loved both philosophy and nature.

I always thought of my mother as being very stylish, proud and beautiful although, even in my early childhood, her hair was already grey and there were many lines forming on her face. You could feel there was so much inside her, so many poems remembered and books read, so much she had studied and lived through; but she didn't have a smooth character. Her temper was dramatic and she could be extremely critical, but she was also emotional and demonstrative, often hugging and kissing her children. She made me feel completely loved as a child. One thing that makes me smile is that my mother, surrounded by so many musicians in our courtyard, couldn't sing even one line of a song in tune and, although she was passionate about eating food, she had never learned to cook. There was only one dish she could prepare by herself. Boiling some water in a pan, she would cook a little pork with some finely chopped spring onion and star anise. Then, slicing the meat, which she loved, very finely, she would dip each slice into a bowl of soy sauce, accompanied by some steamed rice. At the same time, she would add some salt and ginger to the water in which the pork had been cooked, and drink this as a soup. Delicious, she said!

Another dish that my mother loved, but relied on my sisters to cook for her, was *hong shao zhu ti* (red stewed pig's trotters), a delicacy in Chinese home cooking. These were occasionally available to buy with our ration tickets in the bigger grocery shop, further down the street, and my sisters felt so lucky if they were among the first in the queue to buy two or three trotters to make this traditional dish. Absorbing all the flavours of ginger, garlic, spring onion, star anise, soy sauce and cooking rice wine during the *shao* process, in which the liquid simmers for a long time and is reduced, the skin and fragments of lean meat became extremely tasty and, so my mother believed, were highly nutritious. She also loved to eat pig's heart, intestines, kidney or liver, which my sisters would marinade in rice wine with a little cornflour, before frying quickly over a high heat to create different tastes and textures. I thought my mother a little eccentric in her tastes.

In her fascination with foreign languages and literature, her belief in the importance of education and her strength of character, she was none the less a modern woman. She was not religious at all; instead I think her spirituality found expression through her love of poetry and nature. She was always reciting lines of poetry in our home, or talking about the nature that she loved, especially the forests of bamboo she had seen in the Sichuan Province when she was first married to my father. It was on a long journey by boat from the

Sichuan Province that my parents had lost their three-year-old daughter Qi (I think her name meant Flag), who was born after Yan, before Liang. She died from a sudden, high fever that was never explained. 'She was so lovely, Xiao Yue,' my mother used to tell me, 'always singing and dancing. She was very musical. When she died, she looked as if she had just gone to sleep: her face was still flushed from the fever and she was so still, so beautiful. But we had to continue on our journey. We had to leave her. My little ballerina.' Returning to the boat, she had written a poem to Qi, which she kept throughout her life. I think that was the biggest tragedy for my mother, more than all the suffering that was to come.

'Xiao Yue, come here,' my mother would say when she wanted to talk to me. 'Bamboo is the strongest material, you know, even stronger than metal. It is like the Eastern character: it can suffer so much, but it is not broken because it can bend. Look how one piece of bamboo can support two full buckets of water, across the shoulders of one man. The bamboo bends but does not break.' I would listen impatiently, wanting to return to my games in the alleys, not really understanding her words. I was too little to appreciate this sophisticated woman who was my mother: I couldn't really communicate with her.

Bamboo was also one of my mother's favourite foods. She would buy stewed bamboo shoots when I was little, preserved in oil, which had a fresh taste and were very cheap to buy in the grocery shop at the end of our alley. She loved all bamboo dishes, but especially a symbolic one called *zheng-zi*, literally meaning 'plant next generation son'. Bamboo leaves would be wrapped around sticky rice, with two or three dried dates in the centre of the rice, the package tied with natural string from the bamboo leaves and then steamed. These parcels, which must originally have symbolised fertility, could be bought ready-made during an annual festival called Zheng-zi Day, in memory of a Chinese hero from the old days named

Qu Yuan. A poet and one of the emperor's highest ministers, he had tried to change the political system, which was very corrupt. But finding change impossible, he had walked into a lake and drowned himself. People remembered him by throwing these bamboo parcels into a lake. I loved *zheng-zi* so much because the smell of the steamed rice, which had absorbed the scent of the bamboo, was delicious. Using chopsticks, I would dip the sticky rice into sugar and eat it, keeping the dates until last. We could only eat them during this festival time, once a year, which made the taste all the more intense. Each family would be given special ration tickets which they could use either to buy them freshly made or to purchase the ingredients to make their own: the unique sticky rice and bamboo leaves from the south of China.

Another festival which my mother loved to celebrate was the annual Moon Festival, when every family would come together to eat moon cake. It is a traditional autumn festival, in September or October, which follows the Chinese lunar calendar and coincides with a full moon. The cake itself, round like the moon, consists of a thick pastry case made from white wheat flour, a bit like French *tarte tatin* but thicker, containing a heavy mixture of different kinds of seeds, sugar and dried fruit. In southern China they like to include meat, egg yolk and nuts in their moon cake but, in the north of China, we like the simple, sweet version with walnuts and almonds. When I was young we could sometimes only afford the cheapest moon cake: called *bai tang*, it is simply stuffed with white sugar. Actually this was, and still is, my favourite moon cake, but is no longer made. The most important part of the Moon Festival was *tuan yuan* (meaning 'get together in a circle'). My mother used to say, 'Even if your son is on the edge of the world, the family must still get together to look at the moon.' Standing outside our rooms on the evening of the Moon Festival, we would listen to the musicians of our courtyard playing traditional melodies, among them 'Moon Reflections on the Lake'. This piece had been written by a blind man, an *erhu* player called A Bing, two or three hundred years before. He had travelled around the countryside, performing for the wealthy landlords and had composed this melody for the Moon Festival celebrations. I remember my father sometimes playing this sad tune in the courtyard. It was part of the repertoire for all *erhu* players.

Of course, the most important festival in the alleys, and throughout the whole of China when I was little, was Chun Jie, meaning Spring Festival, our Chinese New Year, which follows the lunar calendar, a time in which my mother was always happy. It marked the end of winter and the beginning of spring, of families getting together and eating dumplings; and in my courtyard this meant a lot of music too. From midday on New Year's Eve, the first of three festival days, my sisters began to make dumplings, rolling the dough, making the stuffing, forming the intricate folds which meant that the

37

jiaozi would keep their shape when boiled. Before our *jiaozi* we would eat 'thousand-year eggs', duck eggs which have been buried in lime for many days to give them a distinctive taste and colour, and then steamed or hard boiled. We would eat these as a starter, cut in half and served with finely chopped garlic and a few drops of soy sauce and sesame seed oil. Then, after eating our steaming dumplings, our faces flushed with their heat and our excitement, the fireworks began to sound in the alleys and neighbouring courtyards. Every family could afford to buy a few single fireworks or firecrackers, which were very cheap; and companies would also give these as free gifts to their workers. My mother used to give me a little red fire-cracker which came in a packet. Inside there were four interwoven firecrackers, the length of matchsticks, which you were supposed to put on to the end of a bamboo stick and then light. But, like the other children in the alley, I didn't want mine to be over in one go, so I used to separate them, lighting each one individually with the end of an incense stick. Once alight, I threw each one into the sky, or over our courtyard wall, delighting in the sound and the red colour that lit up the sky. They were so small, they weren't dangerous. At that moment, after the whole city had eaten their dumplings, the alleys themselves seemed to vibrate with the sound of fireworks and the sky was red for many hours.

Inside people's homes and courtyards, there was a lot of singing, laughing and dancing. I don't remember my family talking very much about whether it was the year of the Horse, the Snake (we say Little Dragon), the Pig or the Monkey, for example, although the year of the Dragon, my mother's year, was always considered special. If it was your year, you were supposed to wear a red cotton belt to ensure that you would have a good 12 months, that you would be lucky. But mostly the talk was about eating, not spiritual things. The government wanted people to enjoy the Spring Festival and every family was given extra rations to buy enough good food to last for one to two weeks: sunflower seeds and cooked peanuts in their shells, some extra pork and even some fish. To have this extra food was such a wonderful feeling; we were all very happy. I remember my first sister Kai especially loved the sunflower seeds, and still does to this day. She can eat them at high speed, like a hungry squirrel, nibbling all around the edge and then twisting the kernel, taking the seed out with the tip of her tongue. She can eat perhaps a hundred of these at the end of a meal, drinking copious amounts of jasmine tea and, as her conversation gets more heated, so the mountain of seed kernels grows higher and higher!

The next morning was traditionally known as 'visiting day'. As I walked through the alley with my family, going into neighbouring courtyards, I could hardly see the grey earth on the ground: it was covered with all the little red and yellow papers from the fireworks and firecrackers that had filled the sky. I loved that feeling. On the streets that day, they were selling fresh fruit sticks for children and my mother used to buy one for me. They were covered in caramelised sugar and were icy cold, so the outside was crisp, the inside fresh.

RECIPE

- *Mu xu cai* (woodland dish): bamboo shoots, lily flower, wood ear, dried mushrooms *see pages* 194–6

Chapter 7

PLAYING BY THE RIVER

Educated as she was, my mother remained a little super-
stitious throughout her life. I sometimes accompanied
her to a traditional medicine shop, with many steps leading
up to the door, where hundreds of different herbs and plants
were kept in countless tiny, labelled wooden drawers. My
mother used to return to the courtyard with a brown paper
parcel in her hand, tied with string. She would boil these
plants for many hours, creating a liquid that tasted horrible.
But the Chinese believe, the nastier the taste, the more effec-
tive the medicine. When my father was very ill, towards the
end of his life, she used to brew his medicine in this way and
then, taking the herbs and plants out of the pan, she would
ask my sisters to lay them on the ground in the alley, outside
our courtyard. As people's feet and bicycle wheels flattened
the plants into the earth, the traditional belief was that the
illness would be forced out of the patient's body. My mother
told me that what my father had needed most, when he was
so thin and in such pain, was just some good nutrition, a fresh
egg or an apple, which he kept asking for at the end. But she

could give him neither. After his death, she went out into the alleys by herself, returning with armfuls of green plants to fill our rooms with life, she said.

'Xiao Yue,' my mother said to me, 'if you have a problem and you cannot find the answer, go to the river to think by yourself. You will find quietness there, and nature will give you inspiration.' My mother never spoke to me about religion. God was not allowed in my childhood; but we were allowed nature.

Hu Cheng He, meaning 'guard the city river', was created during the Ming Dynasty as a means of encircling and defending the city of Beijing (formerly Beiping, meaning northern peace), which became China's capital at the beginning of the fifteenth century. Over hundreds of years this river, which was slightly bending, had become more natural, with banks of dark earth and willow trees. We used to play on what remained of the Cheng Qiang, the old city wall. I remember the big, grey stones from this wall were often taken by people in the alleys to build little outside kitchens in their courtyards. On my side of the riverbank, which was known as *cheng li* (inside the city), there was a line of tall, thin trees called *yang shu*, with whitish-coloured bark and green, heart-shaped leaves. The trunks were so straight that they seemed to go right up into the sky, and I always thought how beautiful they

were. The water in the river was exceptionally clear in those days, so you could see many stones and fish. We used to catch these little river fish, standing completely still in the water and using our hands. There were also frogs to catch, and dragonflies, many of them flying just above the surface of the water.

Someone in the alley had told my friend Xiao-Xiao, the son of one of the wind musicians in our courtyard and my best friend, that if you drank a handful of tadpoles from the river, you would develop unusually good eyesight. I thought it much more likely that they would turn into frogs inside my tummy but still I drank some, not wanting to lose face, and secretly hoping that from that day I would have exceptionally bright, clear eyes.

Sometimes we would go to the river to catch the tiny yellow birds that flew among the branches of the trees. We used to try imitating the patterns of their song with whistles and, as children of musicians, we became so good at this that the birds really seemed to answer us. To catch one you needed to bring a bamboo chopstick, a metal basin (the kind we used for washing our faces), some string and a few grains of uncooked rice. Tying a long piece of string to the middle

With my good friend Xiao-Xiao in our courtyard, aged 6 or 7

of the chopstick, you put the grains of rice underneath the basin which was supported by one end of the chopstick, creating a space for the bird to enter. Hiding behind the riverbank, you would wait until a bird began eating the grains of rice, then you would pull the string, trapping it beneath the basin. If Xiao-Xiao caught a bird, he would take it home to the courtyard and keep it in a cage. But although I felt so clever to be able to catch something wild and free, I didn't like the idea of keeping it, of taking away its freedom altogether. I would try to feed it with grains of rice, but feeling the rhythm of its heart beating against my hand, I would always let it go.

Chapter 8

COOKING WITH
MY SISTERS

For breakfast, everyone in our courtyard would eat rice soup, which was very bland and had the texture of porridge, accompanied by pickles, called *da jiang luoba*. Made from a large fresh vegetable called *shui luoba*, which is shaped like an aubergine and belongs to the carrot family, these thin pieces of pickled vegetable were kept in a clay pot in the grocery shop near the end of our alley. They were wrapped in rough brown paper and, just carrying this package home, you would already begin to feel salty; you could only eat a little at a time. They were also sold with sesame seeds and chilli added to them but these were a lot more expensive.

Sitting over breakfast each morning my sisters would ask each other, '*Jin-tian che shan mo?* (what shall we eat today?).' By the beginning of 1966, the economy in China was slowly beginning to improve and we had a little more food to eat, although certain ingredients, such as sesame seed oil, sesame seed paste, pork, eggs and *dou-fu* (fresh bean curd, made from yellow soy beans), which in China is considered to be one of the best ingredients for your health, were still highly rationed.

So my family's choice of dishes still depended on the supply of fresh, seasonal vegetables produced by farmers in the countryside. During the winter, these were limited to potatoes, cabbage and *bai-cai*, which we would heap in piles outside our door in the courtyard to stay fresh for many days in the intense cold. To add variety to these extremely limited ingredients we would have pickled vegetables, which were not rationed, a small amount of pork and a little of the highly rationed dried or preserved ingredients, such as dried lily flower and wood ear (a kind of tree fungus), bamboo shoots preserved in oil, dried bamboo sheets and dried mushrooms. In the summer, there were many more colourful vegetables available – tomatoes, cucumbers, radishes, squashes, cauliflowers, yellow and green beansprouts, onions and green beans. You could also find *jiu-cai* (a thin, green and grasslike vegetable with a strong taste, like something between garlic and spring onion), *jiu-huang* (thin, yellow and grasslike, with a milder taste), *xiao bai-cai* (a green leaf vegetable), *bo-cai* (spinach), and of course aubergines – hundreds of them arranged in piles of deep purple on the grey earth outside the grocery shop. But we had no means of keeping these vegetables fresh in the fierce heat of our courtyard; so my sisters' choice of dishes was largely dependent on what was available each day in the government shops. Summer cooking was therefore much more spontaneous.

I didn't always go to the river with my friends. Sometimes I just played games in the alleys. We used to collect apricot stones whenever we were given an apricot to eat or we would pick up the stones that people had thrown on the ground after eating the fruit. When we had collected enough, we could begin to play our game. Making five smooth holes in the earth of the alley, we would place one apricot stone in the first hole, two in the second, three in the third, and so on. Then, taking turns, we would throw an apricot stone into the first hole, aiming to hit the stone out of the hole; then we would do the same with the next hole. The boy who could hit the most stones out of the five holes would win: it was a brilliant game, and required a lot of skill.

But often I would be interrupted by the sound of Xuan and Liang, the singers in my family, calling out 'Guo Yue!' very loudly from the entrance to our courtyard. From the position of our courtyard in the alley my sisters would be among the first to hear the shouts of 'fresh tomatoes, aubergines and cucumbers!' as horse-drawn carts arrived from the countryside. My sisters were very bossy of course and, being the youngest, I would be sent running down the alley to get the vegetables from the grocery shop. This small shop provided many things that we needed for daily life, from matches to toilet paper (though this was so rationed that we mostly used newspaper), fresh and pickled vegetables, vinegar, rock salt, cooking rice wine, peanut oil, soy sauce, sugar and sesame seed oil. This shop was called *fu shi dian*, meaning 'less important or secondary food shop', because it sold only the

ingredients that are used to fill dumplings or to make dishes that accompany steamed rice, *man-tou* and noodles; not the all-important grain itself (the rice, wheat flour and maize flour), the primary food for all Chinese people. To buy this rationed grain, you had to take a white sack to a special shop called *liang shi dian* (starch shop), which was about 10 to 15 minutes' walk from our courtyard. Inside there was the incredible smell of flour, which was stored in a big metal container, alongside another container of white rice. Using a metal scoop, the flour was weighed on a pair of scales made out of red shiny wood, comprising a big metal plate and a piece of string with a weight attached, which measured the rationed amount of grain that you had requested. But we would only fill our sacks of rice and flour maybe once every two weeks. Buying vegetables, however, was a daily activity.

I was sent so often to the little grocery shop that, in spite of being very shy to say that I wanted only a little of the cheapest vegetables, I began to get a feeling for them, to understand their character by colour, smell and touch, and they became like treasure to me. Arranged on the earth, they formed a beautiful collection of organic shapes and colours that changed with the seasons, from the earthy whites of winter to the vibrant palette of summer. Still now, when I choose vegetables in a market, I feel like a child in a toy shop: I want to handle each one in turn, studying its unique colour and smell. Each has its own character; each one suggests something delicious. From my sisters I learned how you should use as much of the vegetable or fruit as possible, how the very last bit of melon, for example, right next to the skin, can be added to the ingredients for filling *jiaozi*, to make them just that bit more tasty. It was a lesson that I would remember throughout my life.

Everyone in our alley would be buying the same seasonal vegetables on the same day. The challenge for people was to use their imaginations, to make as many variations as

possible, to create as many different tastes, colours and textures as they could, using the simple collection of flavouring
notes in Chinese home cooking: soy sauce, spring onion,
ginger, garlic, sugar, star anise, sesame seed oil, Chinese
vinegar and cooking rice wine. For example, you might think
of five different ways to make an aubergine dish: *qie ni*
(aubergine mud), steamed by itself, with garlic, spring onion,
soy sauce and a few drops of sesame seed oil added at the end
and then mashed with chopsticks to create the right texture,
a good dish if you only had a little cooking oil left; *hong shao
qie-zi* (red stewed aubergine, with pork if you had the money
to buy it), fried until soft and then flavoured with sugar,
garlic, soy sauce, sesame seed oil and a tiny amount of cornflour; *qie he* (aubergine box), finely sliced into circular 'boxes'
and then stuffed with a mixture of minced pork, ginger,
spring onion, one egg white and some cornflour; *qie si*
(aubergine silk), shredded and then stir fried with soy sauce,

*With my third sister Yan, in our
courtyard*

garlic, salt and sugar; and *yu xiang qie-zi* (fish-perfumed aubergine), cut into long diamond shapes and fried in oil until the aubergine shrinks, with red chilli, ginger, garlic, spring onion, sugar, vinegar, cooking rice wine and a little cornflour added until, curiously, the aubergine takes on the flavour of fish. These dishes are all delicious, but each one is different, in taste, texture, scent and colour, and some exhibit the Chinese love of surprise and humour, playing with your expectations.

'Guo Yue, *hui jia!* (come home),' '*Xi cai!* (wash the vegetables),' '*Qie cai!* (cut the vegetables)' – I can still hear my sisters' voices, dragging me from my games. I used to hate washing the vegetables because they were always covered in earth and during the winter I would have to stand outside, sometimes in a queue of people, waiting to wash them under the icy water from the communal tap at the far end of the courtyard, beneath our tree. My sisters would shout at me if they thought I was not concentrating on preparing the vegetables, or being serious about what I was doing. The Chinese believe that your thoughts and enjoyment of chopping and cooking can influence the food you are preparing, that your mood can even influence the taste of your dishes. If you don't prepare the vegetables carefully, then you are not respecting or valuing them. This was so important to my family, to all Chinese people. Often I was in a hurry because I had promised to go to the river with my friends, to fly kites or catch crickets, which I kept in little straw containers under my bed. But, like my bamboo-flute training during the Cultural Revolution, when I used to go to sleep while practising my long notes, once I began to chop the vegetables into different shapes, following their natural contours and colours, and once I began to smell the cooking, I loved what I was doing. It was like learning to play a beautiful melody.

I began to cook the simplest dishes, such as thinly sliced potato (*tu-dou*, meaning 'earth bean'), stir-fried in vinegar,

Myself, aged 6 or 7

sugar, light soy sauce and a tiny touch of sesame seed oil. My sisters would stand by my side, watching my every move and joking with me. I have notably large, thick earlobes: Buddha's ears, the Chinese say. They are traditionally thought to be lucky. 'Look at the meat on Guo Yue's ears,' my sisters would laugh. 'They would make a very good dish!'

RECIPES

- Stir-fried potato with sugar, vinegar and soy sauce *see pages* 197–8
- *Qie he* (aubergine box) *see pages* 209–12

Chapter 9

A CHINESE KITCHEN

My sisters cooked on a coal stove in the outer room where I slept with my mother and brother. This stove was also essential for heating our two rooms by means of pipes which led from the stove, around the rooms, and then out of the window. During the bitterly cold winters, when temperatures regularly dropped to minus ten degrees centigrade, we kept the stove going all the time with pieces of circular coal which was rationed for each family. The degree of heat was controlled by opening or partially closing two fire doors, one at the top and one at the bottom of the stove. If you wanted to cook, you had to open both, to allow the air to pass through and awaken the fire, as though fanning it: we say *ba huo*, meaning 'release fire'. It would take about half an hour to heat up, ready for cooking.

On top of our stove at home, there was a circular iron lid which fitted into a ring, and covered the hole over the fire. Around this were two other rings which allowed my sisters to use different-sized pans. If they wanted to use a very high heat, they had to remove the lid and cook with the wok directly over the fire below. If they wanted to simmer or stew something, for example aubergine or occasionally fish, they would replace the lid and half-close the fire door underneath. In the evening we would *feng hua* (close the fire), but without closing the doors completely, otherwise the air inside our rooms would have become poisonous. Sometimes we would hear stories of this happening to families in the alleys.

We had one wok at home, for frying or stewing vegetables or occasionally pork, and two or three pans for boiling or steaming, which involved placing a metal ring in the saucepan of water, on to which my sisters positioned a blue and white porcelain plate so that it sat above the bubbling water level. They could then lay the specially prepared aubergine or fish, or whatever they wanted to steam, on the plate to be cooked. Other simple equipment included a steamer with many little holes for cooking food made with dough (such as *man-tou* and *baozi*); a little metal shovel known as a *chanzi* and a wire scoop, which to me looked like a cobweb with a wooden handle, used for taking *jiaozi* and noodles out of boiling water. And of course a wooden chopping board and chopsticks, made from black lacquer or bamboo, which were used for every aspect of cooking, from mixing the ingredients to lifting noodles, putting the mixture into dumplings and turning vegetables in the wok.

Our white sacks of rice and white flour for making steamed *man-tou*, noodles and dumplings were stored under the table in our outer room, alongside little glass bottles of cooking oil, vinegar, soy sauce, sesame seed oil and cooking rice wine. Brown paper parcels of sugar and dried star anise were kept in a drawer, while dried chilli and garlic hung in rings outside on the courtyard wall, tied on with thread, beside a pair of scissors used for cutting these down, and another pair for cleaning fish. This was what amounted to our kitchen. But from this small selection of ingredients and the simple equipment we had to use, my sisters created colourful, imaginative food, filling our home and courtyard with the smells of Chinese home cooking.

In the winter my sisters used to make a lot of soup, which is traditionally eaten at the end of a Chinese meal: *bai-cai* soup with glass noodles (made from mung beans), their brittle transparency changing to the texture of silk in boiling water; fresh or frozen *dou-fu* (which we kept outside in the courtyard to freeze during the winter, thereby altering its texture), with spring onion, dried shrimps, sesame seed oil and rock salt; spinach soup, with egg and spring onion; cucumber and tomato soup with 'egg-flowers', which is when the egg clouds on the surface of the hot soup; or the most basic soup of all, which is simply boiling water with soy sauce, sesame seed oil and spring onion. The idea is to fill any of the gaps that are still remaining after your dishes: we say *guan feng*, filling in the little spaces as though you are completing a wall. My mother used to tell us a story that when the city wall of Beijing was being built in the Ming Dynasty, the workers used a thick, sticky rice soup to fill in the gaps between the big stones. 'This technique was even used for the Great Wall of China, Xiao Yue,' she used to say, laughing at the expression on my face.

The traditional idea is that the soup will wash the ingredients you have eaten through your body and, especially in the cold of winter, will stimulate your circulation, bringing colour to your cheeks and keeping you healthy. The soup is always very hot and, as you turn the bowl in your hand, making a big sound as you drink the liquid, and use a porcelain spoon to lift the vegetables or noodles to your mouth, the traditional belief is that you will perspire with the heat and all the bad things will come out of your body. The soup is so hot that you have to breathe in cold air as you drink it and I remember my sister Liang telling me how once she had burned her feet badly when she was standing on a stool beside the stove, ladling soup into bowls for the family.

I never saw an oven in my childhood: but you could buy special biscuits that had been baked in a big oven, and as a young child I adored these. Sometimes, as a treat, I was given eight *fen* to buy 30 g of these little biscuits, which were shaped like animals: elephants, tigers, giraffes. They were dry, sweet and crunchy, and I would make each biscuit last as long as possible by eating it like a mole with my two front teeth: turning the biscuit on its side, I would move my front teeth around the edge of the animal, which kept its shape as the biscuit got smaller and smaller. I loved the feeling of standing in the shop, watching the biscuits being weighed and wrapped in a little parcel: I knew they were all for me.

One of the happiest memories I have from the early part of my childhood is of watching three of my sisters, two of whom were to become professional singers, cooking together during the summer. They were frying aubergine, twirling around the stove like ballet dancers with a *chanzi* in one hand, and singing traditional songs. Outside our courtyard, in the streets and alleys of Beijing, the music and sounds of the Cultural Revolution would soon begin; but inside our home there were still the rhythms, colours and smells of Chinese home cooking and the sounds of my sisters talking, laughing and singing their favourite love songs. I can still remember that moment, how fun it was, how optimistic they seemed, and it gave me a beautiful feeling for our home.

RECIPES

- *Chao qie si* (fried aubergine silk) *see pages* 198–9
- *Dong gua* (winter melon), glass noodles and meatball soup *see pages* 233–4

Chapter 10

AI (LOVE)

The alleys around my courtyard were always crowded and bustling in those days, with people carrying straw bags or metal washing basins full of the tomatoes, cauliflowers or aubergines they had just bought in the grocery shop, usually stopping to talk to friends and neighbours on their way home; there were children playing traditional games in the alleys; and of course there were bicycles, often with another person sitting on the back, or transporting something, such as a wooden chair tied on with string. Bicycles were also employed in private enterprise, which was still permitted to a small extent before the Revolution. There was one man who would ride his bicycle through the network of alleys, offering to sharpen people's knives in their courtyards; another, from the countryside, selling fresh *dou-fu*; another offering to buy your old shoes or papers to recycle. But my favourites were the countryside people who rode their bicycles through the *hutongs* selling baby chicks and goldfish. You would hear a voice, half singing, outside in the alley, announcing, '*Mai xiao ji lou* (little chicks for sale).' I remember one day going out of the courtyard with my mother to buy some. 'Perhaps we can have our own fresh eggs, Xiao Yue,' she said. The man, who was from the countryside outside Beijing, had arranged two pieces of bamboo across the back of his bicycle. On each side there hung a shallow straw basket containing hundreds of baby chicks: you were allowed to choose which ones you wanted and I spent ages choosing mine. I was convinced you could see their different characters and I chose the three that seemed to me the most interested in what was going on, in the sounds of the alley.

My first sister's boyfriend, Liu Qing Puo, a communist from the countryside, helped me to design and build a brick house for them in the courtyard, with a wooden roof, and straw inside. I gave them bits of whatever grain we had, some maize I think, and I used to peel the outer layers of *bai-cai* to give to them, very finely chopped. I can't remember how long I had them before two of the chicks died; but the last one grew into a beautiful chicken, with long glossy black and red

feathers. I called her Ai (love). She was my responsibility and I used to feed her every day, changing the straw in her house, giving her grain and collecting her eggs. I learned to understand her movements and sounds. She had such a light, gentle spirit, I thought.

There was also a man who came on his bicycle, selling baby goldfish. He would ride through the little alleys, with two finely balanced wooden buckets of water, suspended in the same way on pieces of bamboo. '*Mai xiao jin yu lou* (little fish of different colours for sale),' he announced in a singsong voice as he rode along, never spilling a drop of water from the buckets. 'Please, Ma,' I begged my mother, 'just *santiao yu* (three fish)'. 'Where do you put them?' my mother asked. 'Into the *hua pe* (the flower pot),' I replied, slipping into the dialect of the Beijing alleys (in pure Mandarin, pot is *pen*). 'Please, Ma?' My mother finally relented, and took *yi mao qian* (one *mao*) from her purse. 'Thank you, Ma,' I called back to her as I ran through the courtyard and up the alley, to catch the man on his bicycle. I chose my fish carefully: one completely black, one red and one white and red. I especially liked the tail fins that were divided into two on each side, with one in the

With my brother Yi in our courtyard, before the beginning of the Revolution

middle: they were like fans, spread out in the water. I handed over my money and he scooped the fish into my metal washing basin. I did keep them in our big flower pot, which was made from grey clay, unglazed, with flowers drawn into the clay on one side. The pot was open at the top, which was good for the fish, and I used to go to the river to collect pond weed for them. I looked after my fish in the traditional way: taking them outside into the courtyard, to stand the pot in the sun, to oxygenate the water. In Beijing, almost every day is sunny, whether it is winter or summer: the sky is usually clear.

Chapter 11

REVOLUTION

One evening in early August, my sisters waited until my brother Yi and I had gone to sleep and then, with the help of Liu Qing Puo, they burned my mother's old photographs, letters and papers, poetry books and novels, anything that might reveal her background to be 'counter-revolutionary'. They burned her things indoors, a few at a time, in our metal washing basin which we kept on a wooden stand. 'I am so sorry, Xiao Yue,' my mother would often say to me afterwards. 'I had no choice. You can never know your history now. I have no photographs, no writings to show you. Nothing.'

The Cultural Revolution began on 18 August 1966. The Red Guards, students dressed in army-green uniforms with red armbands, were everywhere in the streets and alleys of Beijing, smashing old things, searching homes and beating people with their leather belts. Beautiful stone carvings and figures on buildings, old windows and the washed-out grey tiles that had characters or poetry written on them: these were destroyed because they represented 'the old, feudal China'. Even the name of our alley was changed: the word 'emperor' was removed, leaving only 'jade temple alley', a name that has no meaning for the Chinese. And my temple school, like every other primary school in Beijing that taught reading, writing and mathematics, was immediately closed.

'Get rid of the four old things,' shouted the Red Guards: 'old thought, old culture, old traditions, old style. Build up the four new things: new thoughts, new culture, new traditions, new style.' Everyone was given a copy of *The Little Red Book*, containing the thoughts of Mao Zedong. Revolutionary music, dancing, shouting and singing filled the streets and alleys every day, overtaking every other sound: accordions, cymbals and drums played loudly, and the Red Guards carried loudspeakers. People were paraded through the streets, in big army trucks, their heads shaved, with boards around their necks saying 'counter-revolutionaries'. I thought these people must have done something very bad to be treated this way. I remember one woman being made to walk through the streets with a board that said *petit bourgeois* hanging from her neck. My mother tried to explain but I was too young to understand. One man had *di zhu* (literally meaning 'earth owner') written on his board: his family had been landlords in the countryside and were very bad, the Red Guards shouted; he was a 'counter-revolutionary' and must be beaten. I was very frightened to think what this man must have done.

There were speakers everywhere: on trucks driving through the streets, in the government shops where people were buying their grain and vegetables. You might be walking through the alleys, or getting on a bus, or buying some aubergines and tomatoes, when suddenly a bell, like a school bell, would ring out over the loudspeakers. The shopkeeper wouldn't be able to take your money or stamp your ration tickets, because at that moment the whole city had to stop whatever they were doing and dance. This dance of the Revolution was called the *zhong zi wu* (heart character dance): *zhong* means 'centre' (*zhong-guo* meaning 'centre kingdom' or

China); the word is made up of two characters, the first meaning 'middle', the second 'heart'. So the meaning of the dance was 'how your heart is close to Mao'. The melody was new and revolutionary, with a lot of rhythms to dance to. The movements, which we learned in big groups on the street, were choreographed to demonstrate the people's love for Mao, 'from our hearts to the sky'. I still remember many of the words that we sang to accompany our dance:

> *Our respected Chairman Mao,*
> *The red sun in our heart,*
> *We have a lot of words we want to say to you, heart to heart,*
> *We have a lot of beautiful songs from our heart we want to*
> *   sing for you.*

Children and adults alike, we performed this dance maybe three, four, even five times a day.

Sometimes the green army trucks, called 'liberation trucks', would drive through the streets and alleys, with the Red Guards shouting out Mao's new thoughts through their loudspeakers, accompanied by rhythms beaten out on loud drums, over and over again.

> *Revolution is not about inviting guests to eat.*
> *It is not about writing literature books.*
> *It is not about writing literature papers.*
> *Revolution is about one class overtaking another class.*

They would throw handfuls of little paper sheets into the air and we boys would run to collect them from the alleys to take home to our courtyards. The black ink was still wet because Mao's new thoughts had only just been printed. I loved the smell of these newly printed sheets and the ink would come off on my fingers as I tried to read the simple characters. This famous action of the Red Guards was called

chuan-dan (meaning 'one by one single piece of information');
it was the way in which the ideas of the Cultural Revolution
were communicated to the ordinary people of Beijing.

Our home in the musicians' courtyard was not searched by
the Red Guards. But other homes in the alleys were. I remember
going with my sisters to a big courtyard in one of the alleys
near our home, where people lived whose families had been
landowners in the countryside. There were high steps leading
up to the entrance, with two stone lions on either side of the
wooden gate. Inside, the Red Guards were in charge, holding
a sale of old things that had been taken from the homes of
'counter-revolutionaries'. There were beautiful old wooden
boxes for jewellery, lacquer boxes which had many hidden
drawers inside, old teapots, chairs, tables, bamboo brush pots,
old ceramics, even a piano, all set out on the big square stones
of the courtyard. They were selling these things for very little
money, and my sisters bought two small wooden boxes for our
li wu, the inner room where they slept, where we kept our
yellow painted table. In a corner of the same courtyard, I saw
piles of books being burned, all kinds of books that I had
never seen before. 'Burn the feudal spirit,' the Red Guards
shouted. I remember thinking what a lot of paper was being
wasted. We could have used the paper from those books for
our cooking stove. Instead, the Red Guards were letting the
paper burn into the sky. They were not using it properly,
I thought.

Only now can I begin to imagine what the burning of
books must have meant to 'literature people' as the Chinese
call them, to writers, academics, to those who were educated
like my mother. I was told about one man whose large
collection of books – poetry, novels, history, art books – was
burned by the Red Guards. The only book he had left was
a small English dictionary, which had been discarded by the
Red Guards because it was deemed to be nothing but a
collection of foreign words, without meaning for the

Playing my bamboo flute, with Yi playing his Sheng, in the li wu (inner room) of our home, during the first years of the Revolution

Revolution. And so this man began to read the dictionary, from the first page to the last, learning each word; and as he memorised each page, he would tear it out and throw it away. As a child, I saw books as paper and ink, with complicated characters I had not learned to understand. To the Red Guards, literature represented the old, feudal culture. To this man, a dictionary of words and their meanings represented a freedom of mind and spirit.

Another day, I heard shouting coming from a courtyard near the grocery shop and I went to have a look. I saw a man and a woman being beaten by the Red Guards with leather belts. Somebody pushed me towards the front of the crowd and handed me a stick. I turned and ran in the direction of the river and I kept running until I saw the clear water and the dragonflies.

'Don't let him go out in the alleys so much by himself,' one of the musicians in our courtyard said to my mother. 'Buy him a little bamboo flute and I will teach him. It's better that he learns something.'

Chapter 12

MY FIRST BAMBOO FLUTE

Hu Hai Chuan (his first names meant 'the source of the sea') was a talented *suona* player from the countryside. This traditional wind instrument is made from hard prune wood with only a few holes, a double bamboo reed for the mouth and a piece of shaped metal at the end to amplify the sound. It is a very loud instrument, used in the countryside for weddings and funerals but in his hands it could produce the most wonderful sounds. He lived in one room in our courtyard with his wife and two sons, Gang (meaning iron) and Tie (metal). He was training them both to sing and to play the *suona*. Every day in the courtyard they began their music lesson by singing harmonies; then they would play long, controlled notes on the *suona*, then scales and finally simple tunes. Indoors, their mother would be making delicious, light steamed *man-tou* buns, or dumplings stuffed full with ginger, cabbage and pork. 'If you work hard on your music,' he would say to them, 'then you will have good food.' With the smells of their mother's cooking filling the courtyard, Gang and Tie would sing perfectly in tune!

Hu Hai Chuan was kind to me, although his manners were rough and he would shout at his sons if they played a wrong note on the *suona*. Sometimes, in the winter, he would even make them stand outside to practise in the snow while he went indoors to eat. 'If you can play when you are cold', he said, 'then you will be faster and more accurate when you are warm'. I used to stand in the courtyard, watching their lessons, trying to learn from them, and I would be glad that he wasn't my father. Sometimes, though, he would come to our home with some tropical fish for my collection, because he knew how I loved to keep things. These tiny fish were the colour of jewels – red, silver, purple, the most vivid blue. I kept them in a glass tank, which I took outside into the courtyard on sunny days to keep them warm. Some days I would ride a bicycle with the *suona* player, to ponds outside Beijing, where we could find just the right food for my fish, little red insect larvae which we could collect using a long piece of bamboo and some muslin. You had to make a slow, circular movement with your net, swirling the water until you had collected this red, mudlike food. I don't know where he got my fish from: you couldn't go into a shop to buy them during the Revolution and, if the Red Guards saw them, painterly and translucent, in a home that they were searching, they would certainly have smashed them for being *petit bourgeois*, an image of the old culture.

But Hu Hai Chuan had nothing to fear from the Red Guards. He had come from a poor family in the countryside, he was a traditional artist and became a member of the Communist Party, protected by his company, the China Documentary Film Music Orchestra.

One morning, before she left for work, my mother put *yi mao qi fen* (one *mao*, the equivalent to half a *jin* of rice) into my hand: 'Today, Xiao Yue, you are going to buy a bamboo flute!' Later that day I walked with the *suona* player as far as the Drum Tower, to a shop called Hong Qi Zhi Dian (red flag paper shop). Inside they were selling ink, bamboo brushes, rice paper for calligraphy and simple bamboo flutes, the cheapest instrument you could buy in China at that time. There were a number of flutes displayed near the section of bamboo brushes, small flutes made from bare, natural bamboo. There was no poetry written on them, as there would have been in the old days, no paint or wax, just the smooth bamboo. We call the colour of this bamboo *zi zhu*, meaning 'golden purple', like the golden-reddish-brown colour of prunes. I remember smelling each *di-zi* (flute), because I loved the scent of the bamboo. Chinese flutes are made in different sizes, according to the different keys: C, D, E, F, G and Bb. There are six holes for fingering, one for blowing and one to cover with the 'membrane' – a tiny sheet of the fragile, paper-like inner skin of the bamboo, which vibrates when you blow, creating the natural sound of the flute. In the shop that day, there was only one kind of flute, all in the key of G. A G flute is smaller than other bamboo flutes and the holes are closer together, making the fingering much easier for a child. The *suona* player helped me to choose the flute that had the brightest tone and most natural sound (for every bamboo flute is different) and I bought it, together with a little packet of membranes.

Unlike the Western silver flute, any bamboo flute can be played by a left-handed as well as a right-handed person. I was so happy that I could be left-handed to play the flute; it felt a part of me when I held the smooth bamboo and blew across the hole to make a sound. I felt free to play my instrument in the way that felt most natural and right for me; in a way that I was not allowed to do with writing. My flute came in a long box covered in green flowery paper, which I loved. When I put the flute inside, I felt as though I were putting it to sleep; when I took it out, the flute seemed to awaken, ready to sing. I remember that night, I kept the flute in its box beside my pillow and I kept waking up to look at it.

The *suona* player began giving me lessons, in exchange for tiny amounts of cooking oil. He showed me how to position my mouth against the hole, how to master the fingering, how to breathe correctly. I watched him and tried to imitate him: nothing was written down; it was the traditional method of learning an instrument. I had to practise my long notes and scales every day. 'That was only five seconds!' my sisters would laugh when they came home, seeing me standing in front of the clock, timing myself as I played each note, practising my breathing. I remember very clearly the first tune I ever learned to play, from a song entitled '*Dong Fang Hong*' (The East Is Red):

> *The East is red,*
> *The sun is rising,*
> *China appears as Mao Zedong.*
> *He works for the people's happiness.*
> *He is the people's saviour.*

I couldn't learn to play the traditional, romantic tunes that I had heard my father playing in our courtyard, or my sisters singing while they cooked. These were the old tunes of an old China that was now forbidden. Instead I learned the music, poetry and rhythms of the Cultural Revolution and, as an eight-year-old boy, I found them both moving and exciting.

Sometimes a message would be sent to our courtyard, stating that I must attend school for a revolutionary meeting, called 'poor people's evening memory nights'. There would be candles on the tables and we would sing emotional songs, 'remembering the bitterness of the past [meaning feudal China], thinking about the sweetness of the future [under Mao].' At one of these meetings an old man was led into the room to tell us about his life as a peasant farmer in the countryside, working on the land. We were shown the deep lines and hardened skin on his hands: 'This is knowledge,' we were

67

told. 'Turning the earth, growing rice and wheat; not reading books and talking about literature.' We were given steamed buns to eat, made from yellow maize flour and wild plants: they were rough and smelt horrible and I felt I couldn't swallow my bun. 'This is all we had to eat,' the old man said. 'The landlords took everything from us. We harvested the rice and wheat but we had to give it all away. And still the landlords asked us to pay more taxes. When we had no more to give, they said we must hand over our children. So what could we do?' 'Beat the landlords!' the children were encouraged to shout. We were told how fortunate we were to live under Mao's protection, because we had rice and white flour to eat.

I loved the red badges we were given, with Mao's face on them. I liked the way they were painted. The dancing, music, poetry, films: I loved the artistic side of the Revolution. I held Mao's *Little Red Book* against my heart and I felt safe.

With my fourth sister Liang, holding Mao's Little Red Book *in our courtyard*

I used to watch my sisters Liang and Xuan rehearsing the songs and dances that they were being taught in their middle school: as musical children, they had been chosen to take part in performances at the beginning of the Revolution. I remember seeing one of these shows in a theatre. My sisters were dressed in army-green jackets and trousers with leather belts; their long black hair cut short and woven into two little plaits, tied with rubber bands. There were bicycles on the stage and all the performers were singing beautiful melodies, old Chinese tunes that had been given new revolutionary words; and they danced as they sang. I remember thinking, 'This is very nice. I like this so much.' They were acting out the present, the Revolution that was happening in the streets and alleys of Beijing. It was my reality, but on the stage. There were parts that frightened me; but it was in the theatre, so I felt safe. When we got home, I copied one of their dances and my sisters loved it. I remembered all the movements and all the words. Afterwards, they always insisted that I perform it for their friends when they came to our home. 'You must see what our little brother can do. Guo Yue! Come here and perform!' I was so shy and would feel my face going red with embarrassment as I began to sing and perform the rhythmic movements and steps; but at the same time I loved it, imagining myself as one of the actors on the stage.

> *When you lift up your head, you see the North Star.*
> *Inside, I miss Mao Zedong, Mao Zedong.*
> *When it's dark, I think about Mao.*
> *You can find your direction when you've lost your road.*
> *You feel light here in your heart.*
> *You feel the brightness in your heart.*

'Xiao Yue,' my mother would say, taking my arm. '*Guo lai* (come here), I want to tell you something.' Only now do I understand the urgency with which my mother tried to keep

telling me about her early life, about the importance of literature, the philosophy she believed in, the languages she had
learned, the people she had met and loved, to get me to see a
life beyond the Revolution. 'I wanted to see the world, Yue,
and so must you.' But I was too small: the Revolution *was* my
world. I didn't want to listen to my mother and she would get
angry as I tried to run away from her, back to my bamboo
flute, the alleys and the river. I didn't want to hear about
another world. I could only see what was in front of my eyes.
And so I pulled my arm away. I thought there would be other
times when I could listen to my mother.

Chapter 13

RED STEWED PORK

My friend Xiao-Xiao (Little Little) and his younger brother Xiao Shi-tao (Little Stone) lived with their mother, father and four sisters in two rooms at the other end of our courtyard. Their father was another *suona* player from the countryside, who belonged to my father's company. He couldn't read or write musical notation: he was 'a traditional art person' whose poor, uneducated background as the son of a peasant farmer in the countryside and his natural talent on the *suona* led to his being promoted in the Dancing and Singing Ensemble. He received a much higher salary than my mother's teaching salary: 240 *yuan* compared to her 79 *yuan* and 50 *jiao*. In the language of the Revolution, Xiao-Xiao's father was described as *chu shan hao*, meaning from a good background (literally 'come out from a good body'); whereas my mother, with her educated background, was *chu shan bu hao* (not good). 'There are five black [meaning bad] categories [of people]', the Red Guards shouted: '*Di* ["earth", meaning landowners], *Fu* [rich people], *Fan* [meaning "counter" or "against", a category that included writers, artists, academics,

71

educated people], *Huai* [criminals] and *You* [rightists].' In contrast, Xiao-Xiao's father, an uneducated musician, belonged to the 'reds': the communists, peasants, factory workers, soldiers. But, although I sometimes heard things said about my mother in the alleys and, although I knew that my mother and sisters looked down on the women in Xiao-Xiao's family because of their countryside manners and superstitions, the categories of the Revolution didn't enter my mind, or Xiao-Xiao's, I think. We ran to the river or played games in the alleys and we were very good friends.

We used to make our own traditional toys to play with in the network of alleys. I remember one of our favourites: a big hoop made out of thick metal from a factory. It had a separate handle with a little semicircle of metal on the end and with this you could control the direction of the hoop as you pushed it along. There were little metal rings all round the hoop, so it would make a sound as it turned. You needed a lot of skill to guide it through the alleys because there were so many corners and on the ground there was earth, not concrete, which made the sounds more interesting. In the rain, of course, the alleys would become muddy and we would have to find other games to play: holding a bamboo stick in each hand, joined by a long piece of string, we would throw a piece of shaped bamboo up into the air, spinning it and then catching it again on the string. We used to practise this for hours in the courtyard.

Xiao-Xiao's mother had little bound feet and her countryside accent was difficult for me to understand but she made the best traditional food, unsophisticated but really tasty, and the lightest steamed *man-tou* I have ever been given: big, fluffy and very white. Coming from the north of China, she made very strong food, using a lot of salt and dark soy sauce. Her red stewed pork had such a rich, deep taste, as they could afford to buy more meat than other families and could be more generous with their star anise, soy sauce and cooking rice wine. When she was making this dish, you could smell it cooking, even if you were playing at the other end of the alley.

The family had a little wooden table which, in the heat of the summer, they would put outside in the courtyard. Seeing that table, I always felt that so much meat juice and dark soy sauce had, over time, been soaked into the soft wood that, even when Xiao-Xiao's mother had scrubbed it clean, the table still seemed delicious: you could still sense all the good food. I remember so many times smelling their cooking, especially in the summer when the families in our courtyard brought their stoves outside, and I remember seeing their father heating up his rice wine in a hot water pot. Using his chopsticks, he would put one piece of red stewed pork into his mouth and then he would wash it down, slowly and deliciously, with his warm rice wine. He made me feel so hungry.

Soon after the beginning of the Revolution, my mother was aware that the Red Guards were looking into everybody's records in her school, to see who might be deemed 'counter-revolutionary'; but I don't think she knew what was about to happen.

In the early evening, I would often be the only one in our home and, as I never liked to be alone, I would carry a little wooden stool down to the end of our alley, to the corner of the street near the grocery shop, where I could sit and wait for my mother's bus to come. I could see her bus stop further down the street and, even though it was too far to see the details of people's faces, I could always tell if it was my mother, from her height and the way she walked. I would sit and watch all the other people walking past, some carrying bags of vegetables or packets of noodles, until the street lamp came on and I realised it was dark. In the early days of the Revolution, my mother began to come home later and later.

There were many stories about the alleys in those days. If you walked in the opposite direction as you came out of our courtyard, towards the Dong Kou, the eastern side of the *hutongs*, you would have to walk through a darker network of very narrow alleys, which was not a good feeling. On the right-hand side as you walked, there was a wider section with big trees called Hou Keng (literally meaning 'behind hole'). Older people told us that there had once been a terrible epidemic in that part of the *hutongs* and many bodies had been buried together in a big hole. There was a feeling of sadness there and many people living in those courtyards suffered greatly during the early part of the Cultural Revolution. There were many stories of beatings and one old man, who supposedly used the pages of his *Little Red Book* to wipe his bottom, was beaten to death by the Red Guards. Sometimes my sisters would send me to the grocery shop in this eastern part of the alleys, because our ration books only allowed us to buy certain ingredients from that shop, and I would always run as fast I could, there and back. It was a rough area and I knew that older boys carried knives.

As a child I was very frightened of the dark, especially in the alleys, and I hated going back to our rooms by myself when my mother, brother and sisters were late home in the evening. There were too many shadows there and the court-yard was dark and silent. Every day I heard stories that added to my fears. In a courtyard near my father's Dancing and Singing Ensemble, a man had been found hanging from his plum tree: knowing that the Red Guards would soon come for him, he had preferred to take his own life. Such stories haunted my imagination, whenever I was alone. So, feeling very shy, I would go to Xiao-Xiao's home and knock on the door. His home was different to mine but I felt safe inside their rooms, with the all the sounds of people being together, talking, laughing, chopping vegetables; and I loved the colours and smells of his mother's cooking: green beans fried with garlic and soy sauce; aubergine silk with garlic, soy sauce and sesame seed oil; *hong shao dai yu* (red stewed belt fish) and *hong shao rou* (red stewed pork), cooked for a long time in dark soy sauce and cooking rice wine. Usually, Xiao-Xiao's mother took little notice of me as she cooked and the family ate together but sometimes she would hand me a piece of hot white steamed *man-tou* with a small piece of pork, flavoured with star anise and ginger. I would eat it slowly, longing for my mother to come home.

Often as late as nine o'clock in the evening, my mother would finally appear at Xiao-Xiao's door. 'I was missing you, Ma,' I would say as she touched my face with her cold hands. 'Look, Xiao Yue, I have noodles and pears!' Once inside our rooms, she heated up our stove, putting first paper, then a few thin pieces of wood, then a piece of coal, to awaken the fire. There was one noodle dish that my mother and I could prepare together. I would chop some spring onion very finely, while my mother put the wok on the stove and waited until the oil was very hot, before adding the spring onion, which danced in the oil until it was crispy. Then I would add a few big spoonfuls of soy sauce and a little drizzle of sesame seed oil. When the noodles were boiled, we put the sauce in a big bowl in the middle of our painted table and some noodles into two smaller bowls. Sitting down together, I would use a big spoon to put some sauce on to my noodles, and mix it myself. Afterwards, my mother cut the freshest parts of the pears to give to me; I loved their pale green sweetness and distinctive scent. I wanted to talk to my mother, to tell her that I had been practising my flute, that I had found some crickets down by the river, that I had been eating pork and *man-tou* in Xiao-Xiao's home. But my mother was too tired to talk very much and no longer told me what was happening in her school.

RECIPE

• *Hong shao rou* (red stewed pork) *see pages* 206–9

Chapter 14

DARKNESS

One evening, when my sisters were at home, a note was sent to our courtyard, saying that my mother should be collected from her school. When my sisters brought my mother home, there was black ink in her silver hair and salt in her wounds. 'They're only children,' my mother kept saying. 'They don't know what they are doing.' The Red Guards had beaten my mother because she had been a language teacher in the Sichuan Province: they said she had worked for the Guomindang, against Mao's communists. I didn't understand. I put my arms around my mother and I could hear her heart beating. 'They're only children,' she kept saying.

In 1967 my mother was sent by the Red Guards to be 're-educated' in the countryside. She had to dig mud out of a river and to work in the fields. Each month she was allowed to come home for one night. She stayed in the countryside for more than two years.

Soon afterwards, my second sister Xuan was sent to the Shaanxi Province in north China – deep countryside, where she worked in the fields growing wheat and maize. My

In my courtyard, aged 9, outside the window of our wai wu *(outer room)*

youngest sister Liang, who had always cooked for the family, even when she had to stand on a stool to reach the stove, was sent to the countryside beyond Beijing, where the fields smelt of manure and the farmers grew the most fragrant rice in China. My third sister Yan, with the few English words that my mother had taught her, went into the foreign-language department of the army and was stationed in a town outside Beijing. Only my first sister Kai remained in the courtyard, as a teacher in the same primary school as her future husband Liu Qing Puo. Every day they had to attend revolutionary meetings in the school; at the centre of these was the Red Guards' *da zi bao* (big character report), in which criticisms were made of people in the school. With his good revolutionary background and communist beliefs, Liu Qing Puo, whom I always respectfully called 'Ge' (older brother), protected my first sister, and began to look after the interests of our whole family.

Chapter 15

MUSIC AND NATURE

Yi was twelve and a half years old when our mother was sent to the countryside. Already a talented musician and actor, he continued to attend the *zhong xue* (centre or middle school) and took part in many theatrical and musical performances, which played such an important part in the Cultural Revolution. My mother had always encouraged us to recite poetry and perform to friends and neighbours in the alleys. In ordinary conversation my brother Yi had a stammer at the beginning of every sentence, sometimes every word; but when he performed or sang, he could do so fluently, without stammering at all. We always admired him for this.

Yi was already learning to play the *sheng* at the beginning of the Cultural Revolution and he continued to study this ancient, hand-held bamboo wind instrument, whose origins can be traced back three thousand years. In the time of the imperial court, from the Han to the Ming Dynasties, the *sheng* was played by women musicians, alongside the bamboo flutes, the *xiao* (a long vertical flute, which later I learned to play and love for its gentle, natural sound), the *pipa* (similar to the Western lute) and the *qin* (a Chinese harp, with only a few strings). But it was also a countryside instrument, used to accompany the bamboo flutes in village festivals, for traditional dances and love songs. In China, we call the *sheng* the 'mother' of the concertina and the organ: it is the earliest recorded reed instrument, with a piece of metal in each pipe, which moves as you blow and then suck in air – a continuous action that is difficult to maintain. It is the vibration of these metal reeds that creates the characteristic sound and harmonies of the *sheng*. Consisting of a shaped metal mouthpiece, a curved metal base (originally wooden), which is held in both hands, and a collection of bamboo pipes cut to different lengths according to the different notes, the original *sheng* that my brother learned to play comprised 14 pipes, which allowed him to play only the pentatonic scales of Chinese music (for example, D F G A C).

In ancient philosophy, the five notes of these pentatonic scales were believed to relate to five elements in nature – earth, wood, fire, metal and water – and the aim of composition was to create a natural harmony out of these notes. The design of the *sheng* was thought to have been inspired by the form of the mythical phoenix. Learning our instruments during the Revolution, however, there was no mention of old philosophies or musical theory. My brother studied his instrument at school and took additional lessons from Hu Hai Chuan, the *suona* player in our courtyard. He became a highly accomplished performer on the *sheng* and later, when he joined the Chinese Film Orchestra in Beijing, he changed to the modern *sheng*, called *gai ge sheng* (literally meaning 'change revolutionary *sheng*'), a more complex and difficult instrument consisting of 32 bamboo pipes, including all the chromatic notes of Western musical notation. This allowed him to expand his repertoire.

Apart from his music, Yi spent his time playing football at school, on a sports ground that was nothing but earth, and

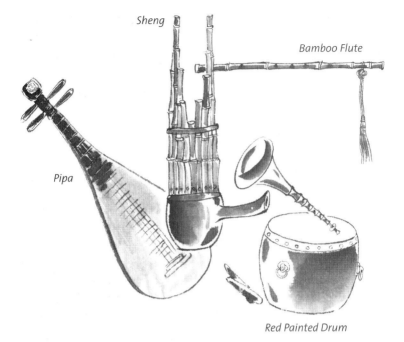

Sheng

Bamboo Flute

Pipa

Red Painted Drum

going to eat in his friends' homes or inviting them back to our courtyard. Yi was old enough to be able to heat up the stove on his own and to cook simple, slow-cooking food. His speciality was pancakes (*bing*), in which he would roll some finely chopped spring onion, rock salt and sometimes a little minced pork with a few drops of soy sauce, handing them round to his friends with jokes and laughter. I was too young to join in with their conversation but still I used to sit with Yi and his friends, eating pancakes and listening to their banter.

In China, there are two kinds of pancake: *fa mian bing* (rising flour pancake), similar to a *man-tou* bun, which can be eaten just as it is, perhaps with a little salt; and *si mian bing* (dead flour pancake), which is completely flat and needs to be filled with interesting tastes. Sometimes Yi's friends would bring musical instruments to try out together in our inner room: Western flutes, clarinets, trumpets, trombones, saxophones, silver and brass wind instruments, loud and shining, that filled our home with the revolutionary music that they played. Other times we might hear the musicians and their families in our courtyard singing and my brother and his friends would then raise their voices to compete with our neighbours, until the whole courtyard seemed to vibrate with songs and laughter. Later, my first sister Kai would come home from her school and cook something for us. Our favourite dish was a difficult one to cook well: very finely shredded carrot and shredded ginger, cooked with a tiny amount of minced beef, soy sauce and a fine drizzle of sesame seed oil, using a special technique called 'dry frying', which involves using only a little cooking oil.

I missed my mother so much, especially at night when I slept in her wooden bed in the *wai wu* (outer room). There was a blanket on the bed made from white padded cotton but it was so thin you could still feel the hardness of the wood as you lay down. The pillow was the best thing about the bed: made from the same white cotton, it was filled with hundreds of dried shells taken from the ears of wheat. Rectangular and heavy, this pillow would mould itself gently around the shape of my head. It was very good for sleeping, and as your head touched the pillow you would hear a soft crunchy sound; it was like stepping on autumn leaves in a dark forest. The cover of padded cotton had been made by my mother, using pieces from our old clothes, which she had arranged in a pattern of blue and white. My mother was no better at sewing than she was at cooking and her stitches were large and noticeable but I loved the feeling that she had sewn each piece together by hand. I felt somehow that she was still close to me as I went to sleep. In the winter, the temperature at night was always well below zero and I was often so cold in bed that I would put my blue padded jacket and trousers on top of my cover trying to keep warm.

In the morning we would eat breakfast together, Kai, Yi and I: rice soup with pickles. Then they would leave for school. Liu Qing Puo would often come on his bicycle to collect Kai and he remembers chasing me around our rooms and into the courtyard, trying to wash my face and hands, and smooth my hair. Eventually he borrowed a neighbour's clippers and, sitting me down firmly on a wooden stool, he cut my hair very short, close to my head, like the other boys in the alley.

Xiao-Xiao and his brother Xiao Shi-tao were no longer living in our courtyard. Soon after my mother was sent away, Xiao-Xiao's parents decided that the streets and alleys of Beijing were too dangerous for their young sons and my friends were sent away from the centre of the Revolution to live with their grandparents in the countryside. I never saw them again. Often I was alone in our rooms, practising my flute and working out how many days before my mother could come home to stay with us for one night. She was the reason I worked so hard on my long notes, pushing my breath so that I could hold each note a bit longer each day. I practised my scales, the speed of my finger exercises and played the melodies I had learned from the *suona* player in front of the mirror, trying to put as much feeling into them as I could, remembering how the traditional musicians I had seen from the countryside would put not just their breath but their whole bodies into the music. I wanted my mother to be proud of me.

During this time, Liu Qing Puo helped me to make a new tank for my tropical fish, using metal and glass, sealing the edges with careful precision. He always had a lot of patience for practical things. I loved to sit and watch the moving colours of the fish; they seemed to be good at waiting, helping each other through moments of loneliness and they helped me too. Just observing them gave me a beautiful feeling. I kept goldfish too, inside our rooms in the winter, outside in the heat of summer, decorating our courtyard alongside the yellow sunflowers, which grew tall and vibrant against the wall.

I still went to the river, sometimes with Gang and Tie, the sons of Hu Hai Chuan. Before the beginning of the Cultural Revolution, it was a tradition for both adults and children to fly kites in Tiananmen Square, about one hour's walk from our courtyard. Traditional kites in China were made from paper of many different colours, with paintings and poetry as decoration. But from 1966 the flying of kites, a symbol of the old culture and certainly a powerful image of spiritual freedom, was banned by the Red Guards. I think they also believed that 'counter-revolutionary' words or messages might be written on the tails of a kite and passed on freely by the wind. But the Red Guards were not interested in nine-year-old boys and would never have thought to follow us to the river.

To make a kite, I used to take a few sheets of my mother's white writing paper, which she had bought from the shop with the yellow door, the same shop where she had bought my calligraphy brush and ink stone. This paper was very thin – perfect for making a kite. I would stick two strips of bamboo in the shape of a cross on to one side of the sheet of paper, using glue which I made myself by stirring a little flour into a little boiling water; this was enough to hold the light bamboo in place. I didn't paint my kite at all: it was just white. I would then make the thin paper tails of the kite by cutting a number of white paper strips and sticking them together: the tails had to be long enough to balance the kite. Sometimes I made two tails, sometimes three; or sometimes I would link two tails together with some glue. We used to make our kites at home and then meet at the river, to see them fly. I loved these pure white kites. It was a beautiful, exhilarating feeling to let them fly high above the river, free and dancing in the wind. Looking up into the sky, feeling the string tugging at my hand, their lightness gave me strength. We used to compete with each other, to see whose kite could fly the highest.

Sometimes, Kai gave me a little money of my own to buy a piece of fresh sugar cane, to take with me to the river. First, you had to peel it with your teeth and then, when you bit the inside, the texture was like coconut and the juice was like a sweet fruit juice. It was cheap to buy and was one of the few sweet things I had to eat as a child. Chocolate was unknown in the alleys; even now, it tastes like medicine to me!

If I was alone in the brightness of the mornings, I liked to go to the river by myself, to catch dragonflies. Before I left the courtyard, I would take some of my rubber bands which I used to collect in the alleys, and melt them over the fire of our stove, using a metal spoon; this smelt really horrible but made them sticky enough to mould into a ball of rubber. I had to do this just before I was going to the river, so that the rubber ball would be just the right consistency to stick on to the end of a long bamboo stick. After flying just above the surface of the water, catching insects, dragonflies always come to rest on the branch of a tree. Waiting for that moment, I would guide my bamboo stick towards a dragonfly: you had to be very still and accurate to do this because dragonflies are very quick, very aware. You had to stick the rubber ball on to the dragonfly's back, not its wings, otherwise it couldn't fly again. Once I had caught my dragonfly, I would fold the wings up gently with my fingers, remove the rubber ball from its back, and put the head, with its face like a clear crystal ball, in-between two of my fingers so that it couldn't move. Using this method, I could catch four dragonflies at a time, taking them back to my courtyard in one hand.

Once inside our home, I tried to train them. Taking them to one end of the room I would say 'Fly!' and they would fly across the room to our net curtains where they would just sit. I really felt that I was training them, that they were listening

to me and doing what I wanted them to do. But I would only keep them for a day or two. After training I would take my dragonflies through the courtyard, out into the alley and, aiming them in the direction of the river, I would open my fingers and let them be free.

On the days when my mother came home, she was too tired to talk very much. She had been sent to the countryside with four other women teachers who had all taught foreign languages – French, English and Russian – in the same middle school. To the Red Guards these four women, educated and refined, were *petit bourgeois*: they were forced to work hard in the fields, with very little food, and to learn Mao's thoughts by heart. In her small notebooks of 'self-criticisms', my mother wrote everything in English. We could see that she was beginning to suffer mentally, and physically from malnutrition. One morning Kai was preparing to take her to see a doctor, when two Red Guards appeared in the courtyard. 'Zhao Su Lin,' they shouted, 'you must return to the countryside.' I looked at their young faces, the green of their uniforms, the red armbands and leather belts. What gave them the right to stand there in our home, shouting at my mother? 'Our mother is ill,' Kai said. 'Please let me take her to see a doctor.' 'Your mother is not ill,' they shouted. 'She will return to the countryside immediately!' We had no choice but to let my mother go. 'Don't worry about me, Xiao Yue,' she said, holding me tightly. 'I will imagine you playing beside the river and I will be strong.'

Chapter 16

A SACK OF RICE

Each morning, Kai would leave a little money on the table, usually one or two *mao*, for me to buy fresh ingredients for our evening meal. I would stand in the queue of people outside the grocery shop, looking at the vegetable colours and shapes on the earth, listening to the conversations and watching the faces around me. The grocery shop was a place for people to meet and talk, freely and with lighter hearts, about food. Men and women would discuss the colour of the aubergines, which they chose with as much care as if they were studying a blue and white Ming porcelain bowl; they would argue about how fresh the green beans or cucumbers were that day and whether to make aubergine boxes or save their cooking oil and instead make noodles with their pork for lunch, and a dish of aubergine mud with steamed rice for the evening. I remember enjoying the atmosphere, the open discussions and laughter. People seemed to let go of their tensions in the grocery shop; their faces became animated again; they looked happy. Sometimes I would go up to the big wooden counter to buy some pork with *yi mao* in my hand. I was always mesmorised by the huge meat chopper; its blade was so sharp it would slice with infinite ease. But I would feel my face going red as I asked for a very small piece of pork, so thin that it was difficult to cut. This slice of meat was for the most part fat, with just a small amount of lean pork called *shu rou*. I would take the brown paper parcel from the man's hand and turn away quickly, my pride stinging. But as soon as I had crossed the high wooden step at the entrance to the shop, my embarrassment would be forgotten and I would bounce the parcel up and down in my hand as I walked happily back to my courtyard, anticipating the imagined delights of pork with noodles, ginger and sesame seed oil, or dumplings filled with pork and *bai-cai*, or diced pork with carrot and potato, cooked in garlic, sugar and dark soy sauce. The beauty of these dishes is that you only need a little meat to make them delicious. The pork was incredibly tasty, because it was truly organic: the pigs had wandered freely around the villages in the countryside, eating everything and anything they could find.

I remember one day, when I was walking back to my court-yard with some vegetables, my mind full of the smells of ginger and star anise, hearing a familiar voice behind me, calling out my name: 'Eh, Guo Yue ... Guo Yue!' It was my youngest sister Liang, home for a visit from the countryside where she was growing rice in the fields. I remember my first thought on seeing her running up the alley towards me was that she would have to eat our food that night and I would be given less. I must have looked angry, because she immediately threw down her bags and hugged me, saying, 'Are you not pleased to see me, Guo Yue? I've missed you so much and look, I have brought you the best sack of rice!' Liang still remembers how my face lit up as she showed me the small white sack of rice lying in the dust of the alley.

Liang was 15 when she was sent with her classmates to work in the rice fields, in a beautiful part of the northern country-side known as *bai yang dian* (white goat palace). The best water, earth and climate combined there to produce a rice that was so special you could happily eat it as a dish in its own right, just steamed and served with soy sauce. It was the most organic rice I have ever tasted, bulky but at the same time translucent, like a crystal, with a beautiful texture when steamed. I used to wonder whether it was the best rice because it had passed through so many artists' hands.

Liang had cooked for our family from the age of eight and she used to control our rations, especially our rice and flour. She was bossy and romantic in equal measures. Seeing her watching every movement of my chopsticks or taking note of every crumb that fell to the floor as I ate my steamed *man-tou*, I would get angry with my sister: 'You have such small Mongolian eyes: how do you see so well?' But after we had eaten I loved to watch her singing and dancing with my other sisters: she was a natural performer. When she came home from the countryside, she would cook dishes for me with a lot of imagination and ingenuity. Using the fat from a slice of pork (the lean part might be added to glass noodles or aubergine), she would cut it into small pieces and put it into a hot wok: the fat would become dry and crispy, making a crackling sound like fireworks and leaving behind a residue of *zhu you* (we say pig oil) in the bottom of the wok. Liang used a rolling pin to crush the dry, crispy bits into crumbs which, together with a lot of finely chopped spring onion and rock salt, made a fantastic filling for pancakes. The oil she would leave overnight to cool, becoming lard. If you then put one or two teaspoons of this lard on to a bowl of steaming rice it would instantly melt, making the rice absolutely delicious when served with soy sauce which, in those days, had a greater depth of taste than any I have tried since my childhood.

Once we were eating together, Liang would tell me stories about her life in the countryside: how she planted the rice all morning, only pausing when a man from the village appeared in the fields, carrying two wooden buckets filled with white steaming rice, balanced one on each end of a long piece of bamboo, bending across his shoulders. She told me how time seemed to stand still in those rice fields and how they sang as they worked, to keep their spirits high. In her group there was a young calligrapher, a talented artist and poet called Zhao Jia Xi (Happy Home). He was 18 years old and he led the singing in the rice fields, encouraging everyone to take part in raising their voices to the sky. He thought Liang had a natural beauty in her voice and he began to teach her everything he knew about singing and music. Most of all he liked to sing the romantic arias from Italian operas such as *La Traviata*. 'We are in the fields,' he would say, 'with no one to hear us except the peasants and they don't know anything about Verdi! So who is going to report us?'

One day when she was 16, Liang remembers standing in the water, planting the rice, when she heard a bird singing and looked up from her work, straightening her back with difficulty. As far as she could see, even in the distance as she strained her eyes, there was nothing but flat rice fields and the straight line of the horizon. 'This is the rest of my life,' she thought.

My youngest sister was very musical, with a natural mezzo-soprano voice and she loved to perform the revolutionary dances and songs that we all had to learn. But with the calligrapher, she and her friends wrote their own song, inspired by the journey that led them away from the alleys and streets of Beijing, past many small rivers, to the village in the countryside.

Little river, little river, please go slowly.
Please let me have a little time to wash my face and comb my hair.
We are very near the village now and we want the people to see
    us in beautiful spirits.
Whatever we have to do in the fields, we will do it well.

To all appearances they had written a revolutionary song, so no one would report them for singing it. But inside, Liang said, they knew that it was their own song, with words that expressed their own feelings.

In Liang's group there was another young artist who had come from a wealthy family in Beijing. Most of all, in the countryside, he missed playing his piano and the music he had studied, especially French and Russian music which was now forbidden. So he sent a letter to Beijing, saying that he wished to organise a little group of people to perform the music of the Revolution to the villagers, stating that to do so he would need to have his piano sent to him. Liang remembers the day when the truck arrived and big ropes were used to manoeuvre the artist's black, shining, upright piano into the village. It lifted everybody's hearts.

On one of her visits home to the alley, Liang went to audition for the highest singing, music and dance company in Beijing, which employed hundreds of young artists chosen from all over China to perform on behalf of the army. 'But you have never even had proper singing lessons,' our neighbours said. 'They will laugh at you.' 'I have had lessons,' Liang replied. 'I have sung in the rice fields, among artists.' Liang attended an audition and was accepted, chosen from many thousands of other applicants. She became a singer in the company and travelled throughout China, performing for soldiers and villagers. Based in Beijing, she would often come home to see us, dressed in an army-green jacket and trousers, with a red star on her army cap, her two short plaits tied with rubber bands; and she would always cook for us. My favourite dishes were fried potato, very finely sliced, with Chinese vinegar, sugar, soy sauce and sesame seed oil; *jiu-cai* (a summer vegetable, like long, green, fragrant grass) with egg and *rou me chao qin cai*, minced pork fried with celery, salt, spring onion and light soy sauce, a simple but very tasty dish.

I was ten years old then; and as I watched my sister happily cooking and singing, I realised then that music could change your life.

RECIPES

- Cooking your rice *see pages* 191–2
- Diced pork with potato and carrot *see pages* 213–15
- *Jiu-cai* (Chinese chives) with egg *see pages* 199–200

Chapter 17

PHOTOGRAPHS

Liang and Yan had friends in Beijing who owned a 35mm Russian camera and a simple box camera, made in China: as I remember, the make of this camera was called *Hai ou pai* (Seagull) and it had a brown leather cap that fitted on to the lens. On their visits home, which sometimes coincided, they used to borrow these cameras to take photographs, printing the images themselves. 'Guo Yue!' they would shout, 'come here and have your photograph taken!' 'No, I don't want to!' I used to protest; though any reluctance on my part was in vain once my sisters had set their minds on doing something. Now, of course, I appreciate so much these black and white images of my childhood, usually taken in our courtyard or in my sisters' inner room, sometimes a bit out of focus or a little over-exposed, and often tiny in size because they were experimenting and trying to save the light-sensitive paper which was very expensive.

I remember watching my sisters taking photographs of each other. After the first years of the Cultural Revolution had passed, women were allowed to wear a *tou-jin*, a red cotton headscarf. In comparison to the shapeless cotton jackets and trousers which they had to wear from 1966, their long hair cut short, with no make-up, my sisters thought these red headscarves were colourful and almost glamorous. They would take turns to pose for a photograph, holding the red cotton scarf close to their faces in a theatrical pose that I remember thinking was quite *petit bourgeois*. They were natural performers and loved doing this photography together.

My sisters would stay up all night to print their photographs and I loved the preparations and rituals that this process involved and which I was sometimes allowed to witness. It all happened in the inner room, which was the quietest place in our home: here my sisters had always slept, four of them lying across one double bed with their feet on chairs. Soon we would have an upright piano in this room and framed photographs on the wall. Its quietness was in marked contrast to the outer room, where people were usually coming and going, heating up the stove, sorting through ingredients and cooking utensils, preparing dishes and talking in loud voices. To make the inner room completely dark, my sisters used to hang their blankets at the window. Then they would set up the equipment: a grey, glazed metal machine with a heavy base (the enlarger), one of their red cotton headscarves draped over our 15W light bulb to create the red light and two trays containing the magical liquids which to my mind created the images. In Chinese, we say 'wash the photographs', and this was my favourite part. I loved to see the images emerging on the white paper, as my sisters rocked the trays from side to side, moving the liquid with intense concentration and discussing the results together. They never explained what they were doing; I just watched. I didn't understand about the chemicals involved, why they had to keep the paper hidden away in a box, why the light had to be red. The whole process was a mystery to me and was therefore quite wonderful.

*Photographed by my sisters,
aged 9 or 10*

Sometimes, my sisters would let me stay up all night to watch them but at other times they invited friends to our home, first to eat and then to work on the photographs together. They would make very good food but I would not be allowed to eat with their friends, on the yellow painted table in the inner room. Instead I would have to eat in the outer room by myself, sitting at the *xiao zhuo* (little table) that my father had made. And then, however good my sisters' food was, it was never as delicious as when I was sitting at the *xiao huang zhuo*, the yellow table where we always sat together. I was never happy eating on my own.

In those days, although China was so closed, people still wanted to copy Russian and Western styles: this was impossible with clothes and other material possessions, of course, and Russian, French and English literature could only be read in secret, usually in handwritten copies. But it was possible for young people like my sisters to imitate foreign styles in food, without being reported; and this is what they did when their friends came to work on the photographs. They would try making Western soup with tomatoes; or *huo-tui* (ham) salad – a combination of tinned ham (you couldn't buy fresh ham at that time), sliced apple, boiled potatoes and mayonnaise, carefully made with egg yolk and oil, which my sisters added a drop at a time, until the creamy consistency was just right. They would serve this salad on individual plates with forks, although I always insisted on eating mine with chopsticks. Then, telling me to go to bed, they would close the door that divided our two rooms. I used to think, when boys from Liang's singing company came to work on the photographs, that they were probably kissing in the darkness of that inner room.

Other times, on their visits home, my sisters would make the symbolic *jiaozi* or steamed *baozi* filled with finely chopped *bai-cai*, ginger, egg and a little minced pork which, in dumplings, can go a long way. Made with a traditional rolling and folding technique that goes back thousands of years, *jiaozi* in particular hold a special place in the heart of Beijing people, especially in the alleys of my childhood. Representing love and being together, especially after periods of separation, handmade dumplings have a significance that goes beyond the customary realm of food and the process of making *jiaozi* is just as important in a family as the end-feast itself. When I was ten, however, my main task was still washing the vegetables outside in the courtyard. But I used to sit and watch my sisters making the dough from flour and water and rolling it, with a continuous rhythm and spinning movement, into small circular dumpling 'skins'. My sisters were all equally good at each part of the process but between them the tasks would be allocated, so that a highly efficient production line of sisters and friends would be created, each performing their role with extraordinary dexterity and speed of conversation. The floury dumpling 'skins' would be tossed down the table to the next in line who, using chopsticks, would fill the centre of these circles, one by one, with the mixture of pork and *bai-cai*, before moulding each dumpling, with a few deft finger movements, into its characteristic folds. A hundred dumplings would then be arranged on a round straw mat, before being boiled or, in the case of *baozi*, steamed. All the while my sisters would sing revolutionary songs and I would listen to their gossip. I watched them, and learned. When the first plate of steaming dumplings was placed on the yellow table and I spooned the sauce of finely chopped garlic, vinegar and a few drops of sesame seed oil into my bowl, there was always a beautiful feeling of being together, being part of many people, and not being alone.

After almost three years in the countryside, my mother was allowed to return home.

RECIPE

- *Jiaozi* (traditional Beijing dumplings) with pork, prawns, *bai-cai* and ginger *see pages* 238–9

Chapter 18

YU (FISH)

'Guo Yue,' my sisters would say, 'your name should be Yu (Fish), not Yue, because you love fish and seafood so much.' And it is true: my favourite thing to eat in those days was fish, rather than meat, although fish was even more rationed than pork. I used to be so happy when I heard one of my sisters saying, '*Jin-tian che yu*' (today we will eat fish). I wanted to eat fish every day.

Twice a month, or sometimes once in ten days, fish would be delivered to the bigger government shop near our alley, about five minutes' walk from the local grocery shop. A cart drawn by three horses would trundle through the street, carrying large blocks of ice, each containing many fish. The most common fish at that time was *dai yu* (belt fish), a long, thin, flat fish from the sea. But there were other types of fish that were sometimes available: *huang hua yu* (yellow flower fish), also from the sea, and a river fish called *cao yu* (grass fish), which had a lot of bones and tasted a bit muddy. The cart was covered with bamboo sheets and a man sat right on the top, with the reins in his hands. With our family's book of ration tickets, we could buy maybe two fish each time. The blocks of ice were carried into the shop, to a large white-tiled basin, where the ice would have to melt a little before the fish could be released, using a little ice-pick. Once you had chosen your fish, a long water reed or a piece of wet straw was threaded through its mouth or middle, using a metal hook, and then you could carry it home, dreaming of *hong shao yu* (red stewed fish). This was my family's favourite: simmered for a long time until the fish has absorbed all the tastes and aromas of ginger, garlic, spring onion, sugar, star anise, soy sauce, vinegar and cooking rice wine, and all the colours have combined to make a deep reddish-brown colour. I remember always smiling whenever I saw the traditional sight of an old woman walking up the alley, dangling a fish by a water reed from the first two fingers of each hand.

To prepare the fish, we had to scrape off the scales, using the old pair of scissors that hung on the courtyard wall, beside the garlic. Then we had to cut through the fish, to clean the insides. Sometimes there would be fish roe, *yu-zi* (fish sons) as the Chinese say, and this was delicious when fried. In the same shop, with your ration tickets, you could buy small river crabs (*he pang xie*) and little prawns (*he xia*). With one long piece of white straw, four or five crabs were tied, one above the other, 'as if holding hands' people used to say in the alleys, to be carried home. My sisters would steam these live crabs in a tin steamer with many holes. Then, with some chopped ginger and light vinegar, we would eat the white meat directly out of the red-coloured shell: it was very tasty. The small, green-coloured prawns would be fried until crispy and then eaten whole.

In the same shop, live chickens and ducks were kept in a big straw basket with a net over the top. People could choose the one they wanted and carry it home, still alive. But these were too expensive for my family to buy. Sometimes, at Spring Festival for example, when more ingredients were available, they might be able to buy a plucked chicken to cook; or sometimes friends might bring my family one as a gift, but I didn't like to eat it. I didn't like to eat anything that had wings.

Hong shao dai yu (red stewed belt fish) was one of my second sister Xuan's specialities. In the family, she was considered to be a very good cook because she had a lot of patience: she used to cut the vegetables with a lot of attention to detail, following the colour and shape of each one and she seemed to have a special touch with the ingredients. Born in the Sichuan Province, Xuan had grown up with a love of chilli and she used it skilfully in her cooking.

My second sister spent around two years working in the wheat fields of the Shaanxi Province, in poor, remote countryside. She had always had a strong traditional singing voice: whereas Liang's voice was naturally more Western sounding, Xuan's was more nasal and flexible, bending the notes with ease, using a lot of ornamentation. Musicians in the courtyard used to tell her not to eat too much chilli, that it was bad for her singing, but Xuan never listened: the more chilli she ate, the more beautiful her voice became! On one of her occasional visits home, she auditioned for a small army singing and dancing ensemble, based in the Yunnan Province, in the south-west of China, which had come to Beijing in search of new, talented singers. With her natural, traditional voice, which had so often moved me in my early childhood, when she used to sing love songs while she cooked and danced with my other sisters, Xuan was accepted into the ensemble. I looked forward to her visits after that, when she would tell me about life in the Yunnan Province, about the minority people, their village traditions, music, dancing, and especially their food. I remember loving her story about how rice was cooked inside a piece of freshly cut bamboo over a fire: when the steamed rice was ready to eat, the bamboo was cut open, releasing all the fragrance of the bamboo. She also told me about the nature she had seen there – the forests, mountains and rivers. Her stories filled my imagination.

Like my mother, I loved anything to do with bamboo, which is such an incredibly versatile, natural material. To me, it represented both music and food. 'When I die, Xiao Yue,' my mother used to say to me, 'I want to be buried beneath bamboo. I love the music it makes as it bends in the wind. I would like to be in the same earth.'

In China, we have a vegetable which belongs to the bamboo family but which, like so many Chinese vegetables, you cannot find in the West. A greeny-white colour, with a very thick skin, this vegetable, called *wo-suan*, is eaten fresh and has a taste that is somewhere in-between cucumber and courgette. I remember Xuan making a beautiful dish with this vegetable, whose thick skin has to be carefully peeled away: she would fry it with sliced pork, a little rock salt and light soy sauce. Our rock salt looked like diamonds in those days: you would buy it wrapped in brown paper and it had to be crushed using a wooden rolling pin before you could use it for cooking.

Another delicious vegetable dish that Xuan used to make was *liang ban shui luoba* (cold tossed water carrot): this vegetable is a greeny colour, red inside and crunchy. Xuan cut it into very fine shreds, before adding chopped garlic, vinegar, sesame seed oil and hot chilli sauce. This was a fantastic cold dish to eat at the beginning of a meal: it would 'open the stomach', as the Chinese say, touching your palate with a beautiful taste that would make you look forward even more to the main dishes. Following this, Xuan would make a dish of egg and tomato, and perhaps *tang cu dai yu* (sugar vinegar belt fish), if fish was available that day: a combination of sweet and sour, she would fry the fish in peanut oil and then toss the sauce in the wok, coating the fish with the sugar and vinegar. If our rations allowed, we might also have a dish of *mu xu rou* (wood fungus meat) which my mother loved, using the special dried ingredients which were highly rationed and thought to be very beautiful for the health of your body: dried lily flower and wood ear which, once soaked in warm water for up to an hour, gradually opens to reveal a dark brown shape like a bat's wing. These natural ingredients, with their special chewy textures, brown-gold colours and unique fragrance, in the case of the lily flower, are combined with shredded pork and fried egg to make a dish of earthy tones and textures that I would always eat as slowly as I could, to make the delicious taste last.

RECIPES

- *Hong shao yu* (red stewed fish) *see pages* 225–7
- *Jiao zhi yu* (pour sauce fish): fish with vegetable sauce *see pages* 227–9
- Chicken with red pepper, cucumber, peanuts and chilli *see pages* 219–21

Chapter 19

HONG XIAO BING
(RED LITTLE SOLDIER)

M y *xiao xue* (little school) reopened for lessons after the first, dramatic phase of the Revolution had passed. Some of the teachers, however, had gone. One of them, whom we called Bi Lao-shi (Bi being her family name, *lao-shi* meaning teacher) had been beaten by the Red Guards in 1967. She wore glasses, I remember, and I had liked her.

By the time I was ten years old, we were studying 'literature', simple mathematics (1 + 1 = 2, 3 x 4 = 12) and *da zi* (calligraphy). But all these lessons were dictated by the Revolution. The literature we studied was the poetry and thoughts of Mao Zedong. We had to memorise passages from *The Little Red Book* to recite in class. 'Revolution is not about painting or sewing a little embroidered flower,' we learned. 'You must make sure your heart is strong, not afraid of death. You must overcome all obstacles to get victory.' In calligraphy lessons too, we had to write simple characters that reflected the new revolutionary thinking: *ge ming* (revolution), *tian di* (field), *nong ming* (peasant farmers), *gong ren* (factory worker). The other characters we learned to write were about nature: *feng* (wind), *xue* (snow), *yu* (rain). '*Hao hao xue xi, tian tian shang shang,*' was the saying in our school (good good study, every day every day you will go up and up). 'Be a beautiful worker. Be good students.' This was the message we were given every day. Our uniforms had also changed: we still wore blue cotton jackets with blue trousers and black cotton shoes but, instead of the red scarves around our necks, we now wore red armbands on our left arms, with thick yellow writing printed on each one, saying *Hong Xiao Bing* (red little soldier). We were supposed to be like the Red Guards, who had *hong wei bing* (red guard soldier) printed on their red armbands: we were doing the same work, we were told, but on a smaller scale. Pinned to our blue jackets were red and gold Chairman Mao badges, showing our allegiance to the Revolution and to Mao.

Sometimes our teacher would take us into the courtyard and ask us to lift a big rock from the ground. When we said the rock was too heavy we were told: 'Mao says, "You must make your heart very certain, you must have confidence, you must not be afraid, you must overcome everything that is in your way." ' These sayings provided the only form of spiritual guidance that we were allowed to receive as 'red little soldiers'. Not even knowing the word for 'God' in Chinese, Mao had taken that place in our lives.

I found the studies of Mao's *Little Red Book* so boring because it was too political: 'To lead us on our path is communism. To direct our thinking are the fundamental theories of Marxism and Leninism.' But as a musical child, I liked to recite Mao's poetry, which to my mind was about the beauty of nature, reminiscent in style of the forbidden Tang and Song poems which meant so much to my mother; although, in Mao's writing, the politics of communism was always at the heart of these images. I remember the opening lines of a poem that I liked to recite, beginning *Bei guo feng guan*, which was also put to music in the revolutionary theatres of Beijing, using big orchestras and choirs of many voices. I delighted in the musical rhythms and sounds of the poetry, especially the drama of the Mandarin language, with its four different tones for every sound. This was the only poetry that I had access to, and my imagination delighted in the images of nature, understanding little of the political meaning behind them – the criticisms of old China, its feudal system and religious beliefs. In Mao's poetry, nature represented communism. To me, nature was simply nature, and I loved it.

> *North kingdom scenery,*
> *Ice for a thousand miles,*
> *For ten thousand miles snowflakes come down,*
> *Look into the distance, the Great Wall on both sides,*
> *A little rain falls.*
> *Big river, from the top to the bottom,*
> *The water rushing down the big rock.*
> *Inside the mountain there are silver snakes and wax statues,*
> *Compared with the sky, see who is high.*

Sometimes, though, we were taught lines that did make me think. 'People, only people, can make history go forward.' I liked that idea.

We would often go to see revolutionary performances in the theatres of Beijing: the tickets were cheap and sometimes we could see Liang performing with her singing and dance company. I remember going to see one of her performances, which was about the Red Army's Long March north from 1934 to 1936, when they reached Yan'an in the Shaanxi Province, which became Mao's communist base. Dressed in the pale blue uniforms and red armbands of the Red Army, a combination of choral and solo singing, poetry and orchestral music created a highly emotive performance, which as a child I loved.

In 1969, after my mother had come home from the countryside, my first sister Kai, whom I had always called Da Jie (big sister), married Liu Qing Puo. Their wedding was a revolutionary one. There was a lot of banging of cymbals through the alley and all the presents were about Mao: there were Mao badges, Mao pictures and white plaster statues of Mao which were made in a factory; a 'warm water bottle', which was a special insulating flask that could be used for making tea or washing, with Mao's image and revolutionary words written on it; even the metal basin for washing their faces and hands had Mao's face decorating the inside. There was no food for the wedding party, not even the traditional long-life noodles; and the bride and groom both wore the simple blue cotton jacket and trousers of the Revolution. Mostly the words on people's lips were 'Long live Chairman Mao!'

After they were married, Liu Qing Puo saved up enough money to buy himself a new Red Flag bicycle. It was dark blue and decorated with little red flags. I remember him pushing it carefully into our outer room. It was winter and freezing outside in the courtyard. We couldn't believe our eyes as he covered his bicycle with a blanket, so that it wouldn't get cold. I think he gave his own sleeping blanket to the bicycle!

When Kai became pregnant, my mother and sisters were concerned that she should receive the best nutrition, to make her child as healthy as possible. And so, following a Chinese tradition, my sisters cut my chicken's throat, to make dishes for Kai. They did so without saying a word to me, in front of my eyes. No one asked me to leave the courtyard where they did it, or understood my anguish as I saw her being killed. They couldn't understand that I loved her. My sisters collected the blood and made it into black pudding; then they boiled the chicken with ginger, a dish called *da bu*, meaning 'a big supply for your body'. They asked me to taste it but I refused. I was twelve years old and, standing there in the courtyard, I promised myself that I would never in my life eat chicken, or duck, or anything that could fly.

Chapter 20

PERFORMING IN TIANANMEN SQUARE

In the same year as my sister's marriage, auditions were held in my primary school to find children with musical, acting and dancing talents to take part in special revolutionary performances. And so, for my last two years at primary school, I became a member of the Xuan Chuan Dui (literally meaning 'announcing from one person to another group'): 20 children out of 400, boys and girls whose songs and dances were a form of musical advertising for the Revolution. For me, it was a way to escape the endless political lessons about communism, as rehearsals took precedence over classes, and to do what I loved the most, to perform.

Our music teacher was called Ma Lao-shi (Ma, his family name, meaning horse, *lao-shi* meaning teacher, the separate characters meaning 'old respected master'). He was young and very beautiful, with big dark eyes, like a character out of the old Peking Opera. The songs and dances that he taught us were all about communism and the Revolution; but the theatrical make-up he instructed us to use was traditional and dramatic. First, we would apply *di zhang* (underneath make-up, or foundation) on our faces, then rouge on our cheekbones, eyeliner and eyebrow paint to dramatise our eyes and, finally, dark red lip colour, which we painted on with a brush. I had the impression that our teacher liked boys more than girls; but homosexuality was a word that did not exist in our language. I didn't know about it at all.

We spent many months rehearsing for our biggest performance, to mark the annual celebration of the 1 October, Liberation Day, in Tiananmen Square (Heaven Peace Gate). This was a national festival in China, marking the Liberation of 1949, and we were going to perform in front of Chairman Mao. The main part of the celebration involved tens of thousands of people marching past Mao, representing the three important 'red' categories of the Revolution: *nong ming* (peasants), dressed in blue jackets and trousers, with white scarves around their heads, carrying farming implements; *jie fang jun* (Liberation Army), the soldiers dressed in army-green uniforms, carrying guns; and *gong ren* (factory workers), wearing blue work jackets and trousers, blue workers' hats with studs at the front, and metal sticks in their hands. Symbols of the Revolution, *gong nong bing* (factory worker, peasant, soldier) were the three words, always used together, which characterised the language of those times. As they marched past, each one carrying *The Little Red Book*, Mao waved his hand. From our position in the square, we could hardly see him at all: he looked like a tiny, elevated doll. To us, he was like something from the sky, not human at all.

After these thousands of people had marched through Tiananmen Square, it was our turn to perform, together with other musical groups from schools, including my brother Yi's group, and professional dancing and singing companies, including Liang's and Xuan's companies. Tiananmen Square, an hour's walk from our school, was huge and open, an incredible contrast to the network of narrow alleys and bustling streets that had formed the boundaries of my childhood world. Every school and company had its place marked on the ground in the square – a circle, around which an audience gathered: workers from factories, peasants (in Chinese we say 'agriculture people') from the countryside just outside Beijing, and soldiers, who had all been given free tickets to attend. Our dance was taken from a revolutionary film called *Di Dao Zhan* (underground tunnel fighting), which told the story (the communist version) of how Mao's forces had beaten the Japanese. There was, of course, no mention of the part played by the Guomindang who, under the leadership of Jiang Jieshi, had briefly joined forces with Mao's Red Army to successfully defeat the Japanese.

Our costume was a light blue jacket and trousers, the colour of Mao's communist army, a hat of the same colour with a yellow star on the front, a brown leather belt, and a pretend wooden gun, with red ribbons attached to its end. I thought this gun was fantastic: boys in the alleys had never had toys in their childhood, except those they had made themselves. Before this, we could only search the alleys and courtyards for the right shaped twig or piece of wood which could be carved satisfactorily with a penknife into the shape of a gun. Now we had been given what seemed like the most realistic toy. We were incredibly proud.

The dance we performed had been carefully choreographed. We had to raise our arms to form a tunnel, making blue and red images, creating patterns on our circle in the square. It was a fantastic feeling to sing and dance in that vast space; it was a chance to show our musical abilities, how we could follow the fast rhythms of the music, and sing perfectly in tune:

> *Underground tunnel fighting,*
> *Landmines fighting,*
> *A thousand people ambush you*
> *From every village, every family.*
> *Underground, all together.*

I didn't think much about the meaning of the words; although my mother had sometimes told us how proud she had felt when the Japanese surrendered in 1945. 'Jiang Jieshi was so handsome,' she used to whisper to us. 'Shh Ma, you mustn't say such things!' my sisters would respond. To me it was the opportunity to perform, among so many professional singers, musicians and dancers, on the most formidable stage in China.

After our performance, we all sat down on the ground in Tiananmen Square to eat the food we had brought with us: *huo-shao*, a kind of round layered 'bun' made from a dough of plain flour and water, flavoured with layers of sesame seed paste and toasted in a pan to make it crispy. It is a Chinese version of bread. Inside, we put some cold cooked pork that had been flavoured with star anise and ginger; it tasted very good. We ate these buns with hot tomato, egg and cucumber soup, which arrived in a huge white glazed pot, on the wooden back of a three-wheeled bicycle. Removing the lid, steam rushed into the cold air, as this hot, refreshing soup was ladled into individual metal bowls and handed round among the performers. Later that evening, the square was filled with special lighting and there were fireworks, so loved by the Chinese, illuminating the sky with many brilliant colours.

RECIPE

- *Huang-gua xi-hon-shi* (cucumber and tomato soup)
  see page 235

Chapter 21

COVERING MY BOOKS

I had begun to attend the *zhong xue* (middle school), a modern building about ten minutes' walk from my courtyard, when my mother was told that she could return to her work as an English teacher. Her first opportunity to teach again, after years spent working in the countryside, was to be on the same day that President Nixon was visiting China, to have talks with Chairman Mao. There were rumours that Nixon might even be visiting schools in Beijing, to meet teachers and children, so many preparations were taking place. Our school was thoroughly cleaned and we were instructed to wear very clean clothes on the day that the American president might appear. We were also told what to say if he asked us any questions. We were to say 'Yes' to the following: 'Do you love China?' 'Do you have enough food to eat?' 'Are you happy?' This was Mao's policy of pretence: the Chinese people were so poor and yet he wanted to tell the world that we had a lot of food to eat, that we could be self-sufficient and produce everything we needed. In the alleys, I heard people talking. There is an old saying in China, *Da zhong lian chong pang-zi*, literally translated as 'beat your face until swollen and then you look fat'; meaning, if you are thin and poor, without enough food to eat, you pretend to be well fed and full faced, even if you have to beat yourself to make people believe you. I realised that they wanted us to lie, that we had to be proud; but I accepted this. The idea of going against Mao and the communist government was unthinkable to me: they were like the wind and we were just little grasses.

We had been instructed to cover our books, to make them look better and, on the morning of Nixon's imagined visit to our school in February 1972, I realised that I had forgotten to cover mine. My mother was in the inner room, combing her long hair in front of the mirror and putting it up, as she had always done, into a bun. She was so excited about returning to work. 'Ma!' I called to her from the outer room. 'Can you find some magazine pages and help me to cover my books?' 'I don't have time, Xiao Yue,' she called back. 'I don't want to be late today.' 'Please, Ma. I can't do it all by myself.' My mother said nothing for a few moments and I started to look for the magazines. Then suddenly I heard her calling out in a strange voice: 'Xiao Yue! Xiao Yue!' I ran into the outer room and found her sitting on the bed. She had suffered a stroke, and one half of her body, including one side of her face and one hand, were paralysed. I held my mother in my arms, as she tried to say something to me. I stroked her hair and wished I had not asked her to cover my books. I wished that Nixon had never come to China.

From that day, I would always hold my mother's arm, and walk with her down the alley. Though she recovered a little from her first stroke, she could never really speak clearly again.

Chapter 22

AN INDIVIDUAL TOUCH

In my middle school, we were taught 'to study like a *gong nong bing*' (factory worker, peasant, soldier). We continued our political studies of Marx and Lenin and our lessons on Mao's thoughts. Every day, all the students would have to gather in the school hall to talk for two or three hours about politics; this was called 'bringing the central government points to the people'. In addition to this we now studied mathematics, physics, chemistry and music, subjects that were considered to be appropriate for children of the Revolution. We also studied history, but this was selective history according to the revolutionary principles of communism: we learned about the old dynasties of China and the corruption of the feudal system; we studied the benefits of the French and Russian Revolutions, the evils of the Opium War and the suffering of the Welsh miners. This was our concept of world history.

Apart from the music lessons, in which we studied Chinese notation, I was so bored in my classes that sometimes, when the teacher turned his back to write laboriously on the

113

blackboard with his white chalk, I would climb out of the window with two or three other boys and run through the alleys to one of their homes to play a traditional game of cards. 'Why aren't you at school?' my friend's mother would ask. 'One of the teachers is sick, Ma, so we were told to come home for a bit.' His mother would accept this story and we would sit down to play cards while she cooked something for us. I was always intrigued by the fact that different people could use the same three vegetables in their cooking but their dishes would always turn out differently. Each person had their own individual touch, their own unique way of combining ingredients, colours, aromas, shapes. It was the same with a musical instrument: each person would create their own unique sound, even if they were playing the same bamboo flute. Every breath, every touch is different.

Our political teacher was called Qi Lao-shi. He would appear each day with piles of government papers for us to study, containing new thoughts and policies, about how to build a new China. He would read two paragraphs and then begin to talk; it was like a religious sermon. He would get increasingly emotional as he spoke and spit would come out of his mouth as he got more and more excited. The shape of his mouth was curiously one sided, so we used to call him Qi Lao Wai, meaning 'not straight'. We hated his classes.

Of course, we got into trouble for escaping our lessons, and would have to write self-confessions. I tried to make mine as emotional as possible. 'I was influenced by bad thoughts of wanting to play. I didn't follow the communist path. I wasn't self-disciplined enough.' I remember reading one of these confessions out to the whole school. 'I can't hear you,' the teacher said. 'Speak louder. Begin again.' My face went bright red. I felt so humiliated.

'Xiao Yue!' My mother's face would brighten as I walked through the door. 'What shall we eat?' she would always ask me. I knew how bored and restless my mother was, at home all day in the alleys, unable to teach, unable to move freely. At the age of 55, her life was reduced to going shopping for vegetables in the grocery shop and looking after her plants. Sometimes she talked to neighbours in the courtyard and outside in the alley but they were mostly from the countryside, and she had little in common with them. What she loved to do was to remember her past with me, her childhood in Harbin, the afternoons she had spent skating on the ice, the day she had walked past a music room in the Sichuan Province and heard my father playing his violin, the things that had happened to her when she was teaching English. She had always worn reading glasses for as long as I could remember. One day, in her class, one of the lenses had fallen out of her glasses. She didn't have the money to have them mended, so she wore them with only one lens. Some time later, one of the arms dropped off and she replaced it with a piece of string which she tied around her ear. Then the other arm fell off, leaving only one lens. So my mother used just this one lens, which she held up to her eye in the class. But not one of her students had laughed at her: they loved her, she said, because they thought she was so eccentric, so individual. I never knew whether to laugh or cry when my mother told me this story: I felt so deeply sorry for her.

'Let's have some noodles, Ma,' I used to say and so we would cook together. My mother loved all food that was made from flour – noodles, dumplings, pancakes – because she had come from Harbin. That was the tradition in the north of China, to favour flour over rice. I used to make her a traditional Beijing dish called *zha jiang mian* (yellow-bean paste noodles), with ready-made yellow-bean sauce which we used to buy in the grocery shop. Heating some peanut oil in the wok until just smoking, I would add some finely chopped spring onion, which would make a beautiful percussive-like sound and then some pork cut into little cubes; after the pork was cooked, we would add the yellow-bean sauce. This was especially good when mixed with freshly boiled noodles. But my mother's favourite dish for us to eat together was always *hun-tun* (little dumpling) soup, which I loved to make for her; and also anything with chilli, which she had grown used to eating in the Sichuan Province, when she was happy with my father.

When I was 15, my mother had a second stroke. She would have two more after I left China in the early eighties, eventually becoming completely paralysed and unable to speak for a further ten years. Her body had succumbed to the suffering she had experienced in the countryside and her mind gradually lost its fine clarity. But her spirit, like the bamboo she loved, was never entirely broken. She clung on to life, like the silkworm in its cocoon.

Chapter 23

A LITTLE BRICK KITCHEN

In the summer of my second year at middle school, my family built a little brick kitchen against the wall of our courtyard, for summer cooking. Liu Qing Puo designed it, and Yi and I helped to build it. We had collected the old grey and red bricks from decaying buildings in the alleys; a few furtive bricks at a time, until we had enough to build our own kitchen. There were foundations, a concrete floor and a window covered with clear plastic. The ceiling was very low, so any tall people would have to bend their heads to cook! It was almost like a toy kitchen. Inside was our cooking stove, which we no longer needed in the outer room when the weather got warmer, and a wooden table, with our simple cooking equipment stored underneath. There was a piece of flowery material attached to some wire which acted as the door; and it was only ten steps from the courtyard tap, where we washed all our vegetables. I loved this kitchen, as a place of unusual privacy; and I used it as much for my music as for my cooking, which I could finally do by myself, away from the controlling gaze of my sisters. Increasingly, my mother found the sounds of my bamboo flute too loud for her, as I practised my fast scales and long notes over and over again. So, even in the winter, I used to take my flute outside to the little brick kitchen. Dressed in an army-green padded coat and Russian-style hat, with brown imitation-fur ear flaps which I liked to leave buttoned up, I used to spend hours with my instrument in the dim light of the kitchen, practising my music alone.

Another traditional *suona* player moved into our courtyard at this time, to the room beside our rooms: a young man of about 30, with his wife and two young children. He had come from the countryside outside Beijing: in those days, if you cycled out of the city for 40 minutes, you would already see and smell the rice fields and hear the strong countryside accents. His name was Shang Ri Cheng (meaning 'everyday, up and up'), a very positive name in Chinese. He had an unusual kind of mouth, with a bottom lip that seemed to come up and then out; this was especially noticeable when he was eating, because his lips made a special sound, making his food seem all the more delicious. We became good friends.

This *suona* player was a talented cook. His own little brick kitchen was just two steps from ours and we could always smell each other's cooking. Sometimes he would poke his head through the flowery material, to see what I was doing. He was naturally creative with food, coming up with endless variations, on ways to cook a potato for example: diced potato fried in soy sauce with sesame seed oil and garlic; sliced potato with chopped chilli, fried in oil, with sugar and vinegar. I used to have long conversations with him while he cooked and was very influenced by him. He used to say, 'The stronger the smell in the wind, the better your food, because people will know that you have made it delicious, that all your flavours have been absorbed, that you have got the timing just right.' I found his approach to cooking inspiring – simple, creative, without pretension – and this became the foundation of my own cooking. I watched him, talked endlessly to him and began to compete with him, to make the most delicious food in our courtyard. From him I learned how to make many different shapes from one vegetable, how to create different ways of cooking with the same few ingredients, like writing different melodies using the same few holes on a traditional wind instrument. He even used to time the cooking of his dishes by practising his long notes on the *suona*. But, as his cooking got better, so his practising got worse: he used to play a lot of wrong notes. I think his mind was always on his cooking, so that in the end he put all his creativity into his food, not his music.

In particular, he had a very natural, inventive approach to cooking vegetables. I remember his dishes very clearly. Green four-season, or snake beans, which are long and often coiled when you buy them; these he pure fried with just a little sesame seed oil and perfect timing, so that the cooking process simply intensified the exquisite green colour and texture of the beans. Also beansprouts, which he cooked with a simple, accomplished technique, flavouring them with sugar, white rice vinegar, chilli and sesame seed oil, at the same time maintaining their special texture. Another dish that he loved to make was red and green peppers cooked in a lot of garlic and soy sauce. The oil was very hot before he added the finely chopped garlic, so it made a big sound, and then he added the white part of *bai-cai*, also chopped, and the colourful peppers, with a little sugar, Chinese vinegar, chilli, light soy sauce, a few drops of sesame seed oil, cooking rice wine and a little cornflour. Finally, he tossed the wok with a flourish, to combine all the different flavours, their aromas filling the courtyard. This dish had a particularly good taste when served with bowls of steaming white rice.

But my favourite dish in his repertoire, which we some-times cooked together, was *fu rong dan* (literally meaning 'float-ing on the top, mixed in, egg'). Mincing some pork with a heavy knife, together with some finely chopped spring onion and ginger, he combined these ingredients, adding rock salt and soy sauce. On the top he placed two broken eggs, the yolks still in their perfect circles. This was then steamed, to create an attractive, painterly dish, with a harmony of pure tastes.

Through my conversations and friendly rivalry with the *suona* player, I began to develop my own philosophy with cooking: my aim, to bring the best tastes out of the meat, fish and vegetables I had to hand, by achieving a simple, creative balance between the different ingredients, a natural taste and colour. In our discussions, we agreed that food should be good for your health and your friendships. As with music, food is a language through which people can understand each other and communicate without words.

RECIPE

- *Jiang-dou* (four-season or snake beans) with pork and crushed garlic *see pages* 212–13

Chapter 24

MUSIC AND COOKING

The Chinese believe that you need a little of many different things to balance your body and keep you healthy.
This belief centres around a collection of key ingredients,
some of which have special properties attributed to them:

- Ginger (to warm the body)
- Garlic (to give resistance and good circulation)
- Star anise (to give a variety of colours inside the body)
- Spring onion
- Sugar (to provide sweetness)
- Chinese white or dark rice vinegar (to counter-balance this)
- Dark and light soy sauce
- Cooking oil
- Chinese cooking rice wine
- Sesame seed oil
- Fresh or dried chilli
- Sichuan pepper
- Sea or rock salt

With these essential ingredients, like the notes on a bamboo flute, you can create an infinite number of beautiful

dishes, transforming the natural materials – the vegetables, meat, fish, *dou-fu* – into a harmony of balanced colours, shapes, textures, tastes and smells, enhancing their natural qualities.

In the company of the *suona* player, I began to learn the principles of Chinese home cooking, to understand what I had previously felt instinctively, about the techniques regarding chopping, combining colours and textures, absorbing flavours, making parcels of tastes, cooking in a variety of ways. I found the whole process fascinating, the ideas somehow interwoven with my music. But whereas the tunes I played on my bamboo flute were part of the Revolution, with my cooking I felt completely free, able to experiment as much as I liked, to move from tradition to invention, alone in my brick kitchen.

RECIPE

- *Chao tu-dou si* (fried earth-bean silk): potato with Sichuan pepper *see pages* 200–1

Chapter 25

COLOUR AND TEXTURE

I loved colour as a child, as all children do – the colour of birds, the blue of the sky, the different colours of tree bark and leaves changing with the seasons, the purple redness of a fresh plum. In Chinese home cooking colour is so important, not artificial colour, but the painterly colours that are found untouched in nature, the natural colours of ingredients as they are picked from the trees or come out of the earth or sea. As I watched and competed with the *suona* player, I began to understand that my aim in cooking should be simply to maintain or sometimes even intensify this existing beauty.

The isolation of one vibrant colour, or more often the juxtaposition of two or more in a dish, should be an intense visual pleasure: the strong fresh green of coriander against the delicate white of steamed fish; the simple red and yellow of tomato and egg, accompanied by the fluffy whiteness of steamed *man-tou*; the earthy purple-red tones of stewed aubergine; or the emerald crispness of green beans, timed in their cooking to perfection, to enhance their vivid colour.

Often I would be thinking about a contrast between two colours, but sometimes there would be a collection of different colours, for example in my hot and sour soup, which features many ingredients. You might think, in this case, that the colours and tastes are too many to retain any individuality but, by boiling for only a very short time, the natural colours and distinct tastes – the orange carrot, the dark brown wood ear, the yellow cloudlike egg – each with its own nutritional value, are actually intensified.

Even as a small child, I used to notice if the colour of a dish was not right, like a piece of cotton which has been dyed the wrong colour and you can still see the original colour underneath. This was just as important to me as the smell of a dish. In my brick kitchen, I learned the basic principle concerning colour. With the darkest-coloured vegetables, such as aubergine which is usually cooked with the skin on, you can use a dark soy sauce to make it delicious, with a strong depth of taste, because you are not essentially changing its colour. For lighter-coloured vegetables, however, such as beansprouts, golden-needle mushrooms, celery, cabbage or cauliflower, you should use a light soy sauce, so as not to lose the vegetable's natural colour. And with white or very pale vegetables, eaten raw, you don't add soy sauce at all: for example, strips of pale green cucumber are served as a cold starter (*tou-pan*) in the summer, with just a drizzle of sesame seed oil, salt and vinegar.

The fresh whiteness of *dou-fu*, however, or the delicate transparency of glass noodles (made from mung beans), need colours and tastes added to them. The *dou-fu*, with its characteristic texture, is like a blank artist's canvas: it absorbs the natural qualities of other ingredients during the cooking process, for example in *Hong shao dou-fu* (red stewed bean curd with shredded pork). The crucial process is *shao*, similar to Western stewing, in which the pork and then the *dou-fu* are first fried a little and then simmered in water and cooking rice wine with spring onion, vegetables, soy sauce and sesame seed oil for some time, until all the flavours are absorbed, and the dish becomes a natural, deep golden-reddish colour.

With texture too, I realised that my aim should be to accentuate the natural qualities of vegetables and other ingredients. This is achieved through careful preparation, heating and exact timing, a fine balance between maintaining the texture while allowing the other flavours – the rice wine, ginger, garlic, perhaps star anise and sesame seed oil – to be absorbed. Sometimes it is texture rather than colour that comes to the fore; for example, when crunchy beansprouts are combined with crispy egg and potato cut into long, very thin slices, the colours – all variations on cream and pale gold – are surpassed by the striking textures into which the flavours of garlic, spring onion and vinegar are absorbed by pouring very hot cooking oil over the ingredients. But these textures can only be achieved if the timing is accurate and you have a certain lightness of touch, which comes with practice and an understanding of each vegetable's character. For example, aubergine benefits from a slower process of cooking, such as steaming or stewing, achieving a luxurious, silky texture, without toughness or bitterness, if it is prepared accurately, with attention to shape and thickness, and combined with the right flavours, using the correct degree of heat, and controlling its appetite for cooking oil.

RECIPES

- Egg and tomato *see pages* 202–3
- *Liang ban qin-cai si* (cold mixed celery silk) with *dou-fu* and egg *see pages* 184–6
- Egg, potato and beansprouts *see pages* 181–3
- Three colours: aubergine with tomatoes and mangetout *see pages* 203–5

Chapter 26

SOUNDS AND RHYTHMS

There was a saying in my childhood that you could always tell when it was six o'clock in the evening, because at that moment the entire city would begin to vibrate with the force of everybody's chopping. And in the courtyards you could always tell what your neighbours were preparing, simply by listening to the speed and rhythm of their chopping. If it was very fast, then you knew that they were making dumplings, because they were mashing the cabbage and pork very finely for the stuffing; if they were not chopping quite so fast, but in a rhythmical, even fashion, then they were preparing vegetables; if the chopping was slow and heavy, then it was meat. It was the same with the sounds of the cooking. I always loved the musical sound of the finely chopped spring onion as it came into contact with the very hot oil: it was like a gentle clash of cymbals, followed by the dramatic, percussive sound of the vegetables entering the wok. In China they say that if your wok is not warmed first, and your oil is not hot enough, then your dish will not be successful; it will be like a cold bath.

To me cooking was like a performance, with the careful, methodical preparation, the washing and chopping of ingredients, followed by the cooking process, often fast and dramatic, demanding a lightness of touch and instinctive response. I liked both sides of this process. Preparing the ingredients by hand, following the shape of the different vegetables, I felt my mind free to think about things, to meditate, though I never thought of that word. In the alleys and courtyards, it was rare to have this intimate, private space, this time to think by yourself. My sisters used to laugh at me for this, saying that I probably had a secret store of red-bean buns in the little brick kitchen: 'That's why you spend so much time in there!'

RECIPES

• *Suan-rong bo-cai* (red-stemmed spinach with crushed garlic) *see pages* 205–6

Chapter 27

DRINKING IN OUR COURTYARD

After my father died, my family had planted a grapevine against the wall of our courtyard which, with the help of Liu Qing Puo, was gradually trained to cover a simple wooden pergola, which we could sit under during the summer. We used to carry our yellow painted table outside, to eat and drink beneath the cool green shade created by the vine. We could also eat the grapes and, from a surprisingly early age, I used to smoke the dried grapevine. When you lit the end, you had to inhale really deeply, which I always thought, as a flute player, was a good exercise for my mouth! In the winter we dug a hole in the earth of the courtyard, to bury the vine like a sleeping snake so that it could survive the winter, uncoiling it again in the spring.

To accompany our food, we each had a large jam jar of water from the communal tap in our courtyard. This water was always icy cold, even in the summer, and had a beautiful, clear, natural taste. It was one of the best things about our courtyard.

In my brick kitchen, I also began to experiment with simple *tou-pan* (meaning 'head-plate' or starter) dishes: peanuts

cooked with rock salt and eaten hot or golden-needle mushrooms 'washed' with boiling water, with some crushed garlic,
a few drops of sesame seed oil and a little soy sauce added to
the dish before serving. Such starters were perfect in the summer, when we sat outside in the courtyard. Another summer
favourite was 'sugar tomato', which comprised beautiful red,
organic tomatoes, in different shapes and sizes, chopped into
segments, soaked in our icy courtyard water and sprinkled
with sugar: simple but delicious.

Liu Qing Puo, in common with other men in the alleys,
used to drink Beijing beer, which is very light; or sometimes
the strong rice wine (*bai jiu*), made from fermented grain,
which my father used to buy in the little wine shop near
our alley. Traditionally, tea was only for women and old
people. You have to have patience, the Chinese say, to drink
tea because it is a ritual that takes time and thought.
Sometimes I would hold my mother's arm, to accompany
her to the *cha dian* (tea shop), which was near the Drum
Tower. As with all these little shops, there were many steps
leading up to the entrance and as a small child I always felt
very respectful by the time I reached the door. Inside, the
tea was kept in big square metal tins on high shelves, so you
were only aware of the scent of many different teas as you
walked in: among them, green tea, Wulong tea (from the
high mountains in the south of China) and jasmine tea,
which my mother liked to drink.

Traditionally, women drank their tea out of white porcelain cups, with a saucer and a lid to keep the tea hot. But
during the Revolution people began to drink tea out of glass
jam jars. These jars became very hot when they were filled
with tea, so it became a common sight to see women
weaving colourful nets out of long, thin pieces of plastic
coloured pink, green, yellow and red, which covered the jars
like little jackets. Even on trains, people used to travel with
a jam jar containing tea leaves, filling it with boiling water

from a communal kettle that was passed through the train. While they drank their tea they would talk, to friends or strangers.

RECIPE

• Hot peanuts *see pages* 183–4

Chapter 28

THE COUNTRYSIDE

In my middle school, as in my *xiao xue*, auditions were held for children to join the musical troop, performing poetry, acting, singing, dancing and instrumental music in concert halls in Beijing. But this time the auditions were far more serious and I was given a place in what seemed to me like an exclusive club. It was finally an opportunity for me to perform with my bamboo flute and also to try out the Western silver flute, which was so different to my traditional instrument, more versatile in terms of keys and chromatic notes, although it never touched my heart in the same way; it didn't have the same connection to nature. I received only occasional instruction from the school music teacher, who had taught my brother Yi, now a member of the Beijing Film Orchestra, and some lessons on the bamboo flute from one of my father's colleagues in the alleys. By this time Hu Hai Chuan, the *suona* player who had helped me to choose my first flute, had been promoted and had left our courtyard with his wife and two sons. Mostly I just practised by myself, reading Chinese music or playing tunes I had heard and remembered. I especially loved the music of films. I also loved to watch the older girls in our performance group practising their dancing, using traditional techniques. They were 16 and very beautiful, especially in their stage make-up, even in army clothes.

I had a good friend in those days called Zhu Hong: his first name meant 'red' (hong), while his family name was an old character meaning a natural red pigment; so his name meant double-red!. He was extremely talented at painting, especially portraits which he worked on by copying photographs. In his bedroom, he had a wooden easel and many tubes of oil paints. I remember watching him squeezing out the thick pigment on to his palette. I was so impressed because he put the paint on to the canvas with his fingers, not just with a brush. He lived with his father and one younger sister, so his family life was very different to mine. His father had been a headmaster and was badly beaten by the Red Guards at the beginning of the Revolution: he had then spent years working in the countryside, being 're-educated'. You could see that his mind was damaged: he would sit for hours in a chair in the outer room, not saying a word. Then suddenly he would call out his son's name: 'Zhu Hong, Zhu Hong, you must study hard. You must look after yourself.' 'Yes, Ba-ba,' my friend would reply, before returning to his painting.

Zhu Hong was also talented at calligraphy and was given the special task of writing in white chalk on the 'propaganda board' in the school courtyard. Every day many students would gather in front of this blackboard, jostling for position, trying to read the reports about activities in the school or the behaviour of students. I liked that moment: there was a strong sense of community spirit. Zhu Hong, however, was not the model student he appeared to be: he had a collection of hand-copied books, foreign novels translated into Chinese, among them Dumas's *The Three Musketeers*, Emily Brontë's *Wuthering Heights* and Charlotte Brontë's *Jane Eyre*. There was an underground network of students, who would pass these books to one another. 'It's dangerous, you know, Guo Yue. Don't get involved,' he said. When I went to his home, he would show me 'little people books', the Chinese way of saying children's books, with simple black and white line drawings: he used them to learn how to draw cartoons and caricatures. He wanted to work for a newspaper, he said. That was his dream.

The purpose of our revolutionary education, we were told, was straightforward: '*xue gong* (learn to be a factory worker), *xue nong* (learn to be a peasant farmer), *xue jun* (learn to be a soldier). Every school was instructed to produce something, so we had a small factory making metal paperclips, the kind with springs. I remember the little machine which we used to shape the metal. We also had to spend one or two months working in a proper factory in Beijing. I learned to make parts for a make of truck called Jie Fang Pai (Liberate) in a factory near my home. There were no private vehicles at that time on the streets of Beijing, only green trucks for soldiers and three different makes of car for the Communist Party leaders: Hong Qi (Red Flag), which were shiny black with three red metal flags at the front, for Mao and the other highest leaders; Hua Sha, made in Russia, for the next group of leaders and Shanghai cars for the smaller party leaders. I liked working in the factory, especially when I had money to eat in the canteen at lunchtime. I remember they served a very good dish of red and green pepper fried with shredded pork, and also *hong shao qie-zi* (red stewed aubergine). The colourful peppers you could buy from the government shops in those days, fresh from the countryside, had so much taste in them: they were thin and organic, not watery at all. They were delicious when combined with the pork.

Each year we were sent to the countryside, to work in the fields at harvest time. My clearest memory of this experience is when I was 15 years old. We had entered the *gao zhong* (high middle school) at a time when government policy had just changed regarding education. Our year was the first to be divided into a number of specialised classes, for students to study either chemistry, physics, mathematics or political studies, for which there were two classes. I was put into one of the latter, with my friend Zhu Hong, to study revolutionary art, music, literature and politics. In the *mei shu* (beauty art) lessons, we learned how to use perspective, to do simple still-life drawings in pencil and political cartoons. In music, we were taught Chinese notation, rhythms and keys, allowing us to write only for Chinese instruments and, in literature, we studied Mao's poetry and criticisms of Confucius, how his philosophy was wrong. We were not invited to think for ourselves, or allowed to argue a personal opinion. Our ideas and thoughts had to be those that we were given.

My best friend at that time was our class representative, Ai Tie Wan (his family name meaning love, his first names meaning 'metal literature'). He was highly regarded in the school, with a position almost equivalent to that of our teachers; in fact, if a teacher was not there, he would take our class. The son of a painter who had been persecuted at the beginning of the Revolution, Ai Tie Wan was very bright and good-looking. Whereas my mother was *zhi*, meaning educated, Ai Tie Wan's family was *gao zhi*, meaning highly educated. He knew many things and was always reading in secret: his father had hidden books and paintings which the Red Guards had been unable to find when they searched his rooms, and he used to show me these things when I went to his home, including poetry from the Tang and Song Dynasties, the poems that my mother loved so much. But in the school, he was thought to be the best student: he knew exactly what to say and often acted as my spokesman whenever I got into trouble for not studying properly.

At the weekends, however, we were free from political studies and, during the winter, on bright sunny days, we would go ice skating in the Summer Palace, a group of

Playing the silver flute, with my friend Ai Tie Wan playing the accordion, both aged 15

about 12 boys, leaving the alleys early in the morning on our bicycles and riding out of the city, through the countryside. We all wore exactly the same clothes: a warm, padded dark-blue cotton jacket and trousers, fur hat with ear flaps and blue cotton padded shoes with laces. We each carried a metal flask of cold water from the courtyard taps, a pair of ice skates, which I used to borrow from friends of friends, and an army-green cotton bag, containing an aluminium box. Inside these identical boxes we took with us the most delicious food: *huo-shao*, the toasted bun, similar to *man-tou*, which we had eaten with hot soup after our performance in Tiananmen Square. You could buy these cheaply from street stalls, or make your own by toasting circles of dough in a pan with some peanut oil, building up layers with peanut butter, rough rock salt and sesame seeds on the very top. We then cut each one in half and put a piece of dark stewed pork, cooked with soy sauce, ginger and star anise, inside.

135

Everybody had two or three of these parcels. We used to do speed skating, with our hands behind our backs, on the thickly frozen lakes of the Summer Palace. Afterwards, we would sit down on the surrounding rocks, take off our skates and eat our food, all the time talking, singing (especially Russian songs) and reciting poetry, sometimes revolutionary, sometimes Ai Tie Wan's Song poems. To my mind, the food we shared on those freezing, sunny days in the Summer Palace was the perfect expression of friendship.

One morning our teacher announced that the following week we would be going to the countryside for one month, to work in the fields. 'When you go home,' he said, 'you must tell your parents to pack the following things for you: a padded cotton blanket, a *lian pan* [the metal washing basin], a metal flask for hot water, two or three *yuan*, a metal bowl and a pair of chopsticks, a sewing packet for mending clothes, with needles that can also be used for piercing blisters on hands and feet, a little white towel and a pair of cotton and rubber *qiu xie* [sports shoes] for working in the fields.' My mother slowly helped me to pack my things properly, in army fashion, giving me her washing basin that had flowers and birds painted on the inside, and a hot-water flask that was painted blue, red and white. We had to be like soldiers, to carry all our equipment in a *bei-bao* (back parcel): everything had to be rolled up inside the sleeping blanket and tied with army-green cotton ribbon. I remember how the shoes had to be arranged crosswise underneath the ribbon, with the basin over the shoes. There were two thicker green straps on each side of the bundle and these had to be tied together across your chest with the little white towel. We were taught how, if something is tied very close to your body, you don't feel its weight. Dressed in our blue cotton jackets and trousers, with black cotton shoes, and our parcels strapped to our backs, we gathered before dawn in the darkness of the school courtyard, to travel in open army trucks to the countryside.

136

The village we went to was very poor, and surrounded by big fields. There was earth everywhere: the houses were made from mud and bricks; on the floors there were a few bricks with earth in-between. I was in a group of six or seven boys, staying in the home of a peasant farmer. We slept together in a big, wide, long bed made of thick bricks, called a *tou-kang* (earth bed): at its centre was a hole where you could light a fire with wood, to keep you warm at night. The peasants treated us like little children, making us a breakfast in the morning of hot rice porridge with pickles. The old women had tiny bound feet and very wrinkled faces; they were kind to us but we couldn't really communicate with them.

Mao didn't want us to become peasants, we were told. He wanted us to understand where our food came from. In the summer it was incredibly hot, maybe 36 or 37 degrees centigrade, so we would start work at five o'clock in the morning, when the air was still wet. Dressed in white cotton vests and blue trousers, with straw hats on our heads which I loved, we each carried a scythe to cut the wheat by hand. Standing in a long line at one end of the field, we had to work our way up to the other end of the field, harvesting the wheat while we talked and sang revolutionary songs. I liked the sight of everybody performing the same movement: holding the *lian-dao* (hand scythe) in one hand, you had to gather a handful of wheat with a circular movement of your other hand, before cutting it with the scythe. I still have the scar from where my scythe slipped and cut sharply into my leg.

We had one break during the morning, when two big buckets of water were brought from the village on a long piece of bamboo. The water, which was from the well in the centre of the village, was always boiled before we drank it, so it was still warm. But we were too thirsty to mind that it was not icy cold, like the water in my courtyard. In the house I stayed in, the water from the village well was stored in a *gang*, a huge clay pot, and was used for everything: drinking, cooking, washing.

They had a beautiful method of taking water out of this pot, using a dried, empty gourd which had been cut in half lengthwise so that you could use it to scoop out the water; it was always a nice feeling to do this. Inside the clay pot they kept river fish, which would swim around as you put the gourd into the water. I think they were partly decorative, but it was also a superstition that the fish would keep the water fresh and alive. If the fish were healthy and swimming happily, then the water must be clean enough to drink.

I remember thinking, as we worked in the fields, how strange it was that there were so few young people in the *gong she* (the commune). There were many old men, and women with bound feet who never laughed, although they were always kind to us, but where were their children? Now I realise that the young people of the village had left their families and the countryside to become soldiers in Mao's army or factory workers in the cities. This is why they needed our help to bring in the harvest.

Lunchtime in the wheat fields was always at midday, when the burning sun was at its fiercest. We would sit at the top of the field wearing our straw hats and eating steamed rice or *man-tou* with red stewed pork and *bai-cai*, cooked with ginger and star anise. There was a group of ten students and two teachers from our school who were in charge of cooking for us, bringing our food, bowls and chopsticks into the fields, boiling our water and providing medical assistance if necessary. The students who were chosen for this group were those considered to have the best behaviour in the school. The rest of us had to work hard in the fields. Sometimes we were given the task of separating the golden wheat grains from the outer husks. Standing in the village square, against the direction of the wind, we would toss the wheat up into the air using a big wooden shovel; the light outer casings, the chaff, would blow away. This was the traditional method. The old people in the village used a bamboo sifter to do this but it was a slower process. There were loudspeakers in the village square and every so often revolutionary music or a political speech would fill our ears as we worked. But we didn't think about it: the Revolution was just always there.

Our life in the countryside was very disciplined and the work was hard. The idea was that we were being trained like soldiers, to work like peasants. I was not allowed to take my bamboo flute: no musical instruments were allowed. And in the evening, after a long day's work, we would still have to sit through endless political studies. But eventually we lined up in our warm brick bed, telling each other jokes and funny stories. And talking about our dreams.

My friend Zhu Hong had brought some of his hand-written copies of foreign novels to the countryside, among them Tolstoy's *Anna Karenina*, sewn inside his padded cotton blanket. We passed it around, reading the pages as quickly as we could. The words were written on thin white paper which had been sewn together by hand. There were some characters that I didn't understand, so I had to guess their meaning. These handwritten books had been copied from the two or three printed versions that had survived the revolutionary burning of books by the Red Guards. Lying alongside one another in the evenings, we would argue about what kind of love was the best. To me, the love in *Anna Karenina* was too *petit bourgeois*: she was beautiful of course but her love was so passionate and self-indulgent. I couldn't relate to her world or her feelings. I preferred a book that had been written during the Russian Revolution, entitled *How Metal and Steel are Made*. It is a love story about a boy and a girl who work together in a steel factory and can only show their love in hidden, subtle ways. Their love is always underneath the surface, it is hardly revealed, but to me this was far more exciting, because it was closer to my own world. Ai Tie Wan of course disagreed: '*Anna Karenina* is great literature,' he said. 'You have to admire it, Guo Yue.' I understood what he meant but still I wanted to read books that had some connection to my own experience. People were not allowed to show personal love: we were told that kissing was 'pollution', that it was bad. But of course, as boys and girls of 15, 16, we were beginning to have feelings and to want to show them; but we could only do so in the subtlest of ways, often without the other person even knowing. I was so shy with girls, unless I thought of them only as friends. Ai Tie Wan, on the other hand, was far more confident, inspired I think by his reading!

Later on in Beijing, I remember going to the cinema with my friends to see a film called *The Corner of Forgotten Love*. It was about a boy from the countryside who fell in love with a pretty girl but their families wanted to arrange marriages to other people. They weren't supposed to show their love, even to feel it, but secretly they slept with each other and the girl became pregnant. The village people spat on her and, unable to live with what she had done, she committed suicide. I am sure the government meant us to see this film as a warning against this kind of love but instead we began to question what we had been told. Why couldn't they love each other? What was so wrong about personal love? Why were we not free to love?

With Zhu Hong and other school friends

Sometimes we would go in a group of boys and girls to the Xiang Shan (perfumed mountain), which was about an hour and a half by bus from Beijing. Apart from the river, and the few trees in the courtyards, the narrow alleys seemed so bare after the countryside, all brick and earth. We longed to see more of nature. So sometimes, in the late autumn and early winter, we would travel to the Perfumed Mountain to collect *hong ye* (red leaves), which were falling to the ground. These leaves were so red you could hardly believe the colour was natural and we would take them home to press inside books, and keep. We used to talk about life, as we collected the leaves. We were very romantic in those days, and very naïve.

Chapter 29

THE PEOPLE'S ART
THEATRE

By the time I was 16, I had only one year to go in the *gao zhong* (high middle school) before I would have to take my final examinations. If you were an only child, you might then have the chance to work in a factory in Beijing; otherwise, if you were physically fit and healthy, you would be sent indefinitely to work in the countryside as a peasant farmer. I knew that I would do badly in my exams, that the only subject I could succeed in was music, because it was the only thing I loved; and I knew that, like my sisters Xuan and Liang, music was the only chance I had to escape a life in the countryside. I continued to practise my bamboo flute in the little brick kitchen, desperate for a chance to prove the talent that I knew I had.

At school, after every two lessons, we would have a ten-minute session of physical exercises in the courtyard, moving in time to the revolutionary music that played on the loudspeakers. I was one of seven or eight hundred boys and girls, reaching up into the sky, touching our toes, bending and performing star jumps. One morning, three people came to our school from The People's Art Theatre, to watch us performing these exercises. Walking around the courtyard, they studied our faces and the way we moved: we knew that they had come to choose a new actor. The People's Art Theatre, which was not far from Tiananmen Square, was hugely prestigious: it was this company that would put on a production of *Death of a Salesman*, by the American playwright Arthur Miller, in 1978.

They stood in the courtyard and called out five names, among them 'Guo Yue'. We each had to sing a song, recite a poem and perform a revolutionary dance. Two of us were then invited to attend a second audition which took place in a small theatre in Beijing. I was so excited, I ran through the alleys to tell my mother. In the audition, I had to perform a piece of improvised *xiao pin* (little acting, or mime), recite four lines of a poem by Mao, and sing one song. I remember the piece of mime I was asked to do: I had to imagine that I was waiting in a train station in Russia (they gave me a big padded coat to wear), but the train was late. I had to show as much facial expression as possible, to show my thoughts and impatience. This part of the audition went very well and I could feel my heart beating fast as they praised my work.

It was then time for a physical check, the final part of the audition which every aspiring actor had to undergo before being chosen for a theatre company. I had to take off my clothes, so they could study my body. I wasn't embarrassed: I wanted them to choose me so much. I then had to wait outside the audition room while they discussed my performances and came to a decision. Finally, it came: 'We are sorry, Guo Yue. You have failed the audition for one reason only. You have a little red spot [a broken blood vessel] in the white of your left eye. We are concerned that this might show up in the lights of the stage or, if you were to appear in a film, the camera would be certain to pick it up. We have no choice but to turn you down.'

143

Myself, aged 16

I walked away from the theatre, through the streets and narrow alleys, my head spinning. That little red spot had been in my eye for as long as I could remember. It was the one thing I had no control over, the one thing that had prevented me from joining The People's Art Theatre. I felt, that afternoon, I had moved one step closer to a life in the countryside.

Chapter 30

MY BAMBOO FLUTES

It was 1975, my final year in the *gao zhong* and we were preparing for our examinations. There was talk among the musicians in my class of auditions that were taking place in the 'supplies division' of the Chinese army, which had its headquarters in a modern compound outside the city, about one and a half hours by bus. This army department was in charge of all kinds of supplies, from artillery, guns and anti-aircraft missiles, to medical, food and kitchen supplies, everything that is needed for soldiers in the army. To entertain the soldiers who worked for this division, often in the remote mountains, and also villagers in the countryside, there were comedians and magicians, and a small dancing and singing ensemble, comprising 50 singers, dancers and instrumental players. They wanted to expand this number, which was the reason for the auditions. I was determined to try for a place in this ensemble, as a bamboo and silver flute player. The auditions were held in a theatre inside the modern army compound, where the musicians also lived. I remember putting as much energy and feeling into my performance as I was capable of: I really believed it was my last chance to have a musical career, to do something that I loved, that I was good at.

I had to return to school, while the ensemble checked my records; but I wasn't too concerned about this because I knew that all the singing, dancing and performing that I had done for my school would count in my favour – that in musical terms I had achieved something. Two weeks passed and then one morning, just before our examination papers were due to begin, three army leaders walked into the school court-yard to see our headmaster. That afternoon, he called me into his office. 'Xiao Guo Yue,' he said, 'you must be very happy. You have been selected to join the Army Dancing and Singing Ensemble. You are dismissed from this school. You can go home.' Leaping for happiness, I ran into my classroom to say goodbye to my friends, especially Ai Tie Wan and Zhu Hong, who couldn't believe what was happening. And then I walked out of the school and ran all the way home through the alleys to tell my mother. She hugged me and hugged me, and we both cried. This time it was I who was going to leave her.

My mother helped me to pack my things: her metal washing basin with flowers and birds painted inside that I had taken to the countryside, a hot-water flask, toothbrush, toothpaste, soap and a towel, and of course my bamboo flute, in its green flowery paper box. Wearing my blue jacket and trousers, which she had many times mended with squares of blue cotton material, I left her standing at the entrance to our courtyard, with pride and sadness etched in the many lines on her beautiful face. I walked down the alley, and turned the corner, past the queue of people standing outside the grocery shop and the piles of vegetables arranged on the earth. I felt so excited, so full of life.

After the journey by bus, I arrived in the modern army compound, not knowing anyone. There were about 20 or 30 new singers, dancers and instrumentalists, so our first ques-tion to each other was, 'What did you audition for?' 'I'm a violinist,' one replied; 'I play the clarinet,' explained another. There was a double bass player, a cellist, a viola player, an *erhu* soloist. I was to be the first of two bamboo flute players and also the silver flute soloist. Throughout my childhood, I had had only one *zhu di* (bamboo flute), the G flute which the *suona* player had helped me to choose at the beginning of the Revolution. Now I was handed a box of 12 bamboo flutes, all in different keys. 'Here is your political tool,' the ensemble leader said as he handed the box to me. The flutes were beautiful instruments, all specially ordered from Shanghai and Suzhou in the south of China. I was so excited to handle them. I was also given a Western silver flute, a *chang di* (long flute), the Chinese say. It was lying in three pieces inside a beige, artificial leather, hard flute case, with a silver chrome lock. It was a beautiful instrument.

For the first couple of days, we were given time to get to know each other and to familiarise ourselves with life in the army compound. We ate in a canteen of wooden tables and chairs, with soldiers as cooks. Using a massive wok for so many people, they made just one dish at a time: *dou-fu* with *bai-cai*, *man-tou* with red stewed pork, sometimes steamed *baozi*. We slept four to a room. I shared mine with a *suona* player, who was ten years older than me, a *sheng* player and a boy of only 15 from Tianjin (one hour by train from Beijing), who played the accordion and double bass: his name was Liu Zhe (his first name meaning philosophy). Our room was next to the theatre. It was the first time I had had my own bed, which I thought was fantastic. We had green army blankets with white sheets and we had to make our beds to be like *dou-fu*, we were told: the sheet and blanket had to have rigid corners when the bed was made, like the squares of fresh bean curd I had bought in the grocery shop. They would come to check if we were doing this properly.

We were musicians but we had to behave like soldiers, marching and saluting in unison. Our uniform was an army-green jacket with red velvet stripes – in Chinese we say *ling zhang* (collar stamps) – and matching trousers with a green cotton belt, a green army cap with a red star on the front, which we all loved, army-green socks, and shoes of the same colour, made from cotton and rubber, like plimsoles. In the winter these shoes would be padded for warmth and we would wear long padded coats with imitation-fur hats, complete with ear flaps. If you walked through the streets and alleys of Beijing dressed like this, you would get many looks of admiration. It was so prestigious to be in the army, even as a musician. I was very proud.

Our ensemble was based in the compound theatre, which had a high stage with professional lighting and around 200 seats. The dancers trained on this stage every day, while the instrumentalists practised in their rooms. I used to spend two hours practising my scales, long notes and fast finger exercises. There were also backstage rooms in the theatre, including the dressing rooms, where musicians and singers could also practise. There were two leaders in charge of the ensemble: the *dui zhang* (troop leader) who was in charge of the music and dance techniques, practising and rehearsing; and the *zheng zhi dui zhang* (political troop leader), who was in

In my army ensemble uniform, aged 18

charge of people's thoughts, of making sure we were good communists. These two used to argue all the time: our troop leader was only interested in music and wanted us to practise, not study politics.

We had to behave well at all times, to show that we were good communists; and we wanted to do this because we wanted to keep our positions in the ensemble; we wanted to become members of the Communist Party. But it was very difficult: first, you had to join the Youth Communist Members and then it was all about a certain notion of honour. You had to try to become a 'no-name hero', a person who did good things for other people, without wanting anyone to know it was you. But, of course, inside you did want people to find out that you were doing these good things, so that you received honour in the eyes of the Party. In practice, this meant we were always sweeping and mopping the floors, waking up early to put toothpaste on to other musicians' toothbrushes, filling their metal washing basins with warm water before they woke up, even washing their clothes. It became quite ridiculous, as we each tried to wake up earlier and earlier, sometimes not sleeping at all, in order to become the 'no-name hero'. But at that time, we didn't see our behaviour as ridiculous at all: it was what was expected of us; it was how, in our society, we could achieve an honourable position.

Of course, this good communist behaviour did not come easily to many of the musicians, including myself. One of my good friends, a violinist called Zhang Jian Fa (his first names meant 'build low'), was only interested in his music and girls, especially dancers, never giving a thought to politics. A few years older than me, he loved Western music and was always practising 'The Flight of the Bumblebee' and other virtuoso pieces by Paganini. This was not entirely forbidden: violinists, cellists and silver flute players were allowed to practise Western music, because the scales were good for their techniques. But it was noticed that my friend was also playing it for his pleasure. 'Hmm,' our political troop leader commented, 'you are always practising Western tunes, ah?' For this, he was criticised for thinking 'the Western sun is more round than the Chinese sun, the Western moon is more round than the Chinese moon,' and he had to read out many self-confessions, admitting that he had not paid enough attention in his political studies. Our language still had to be the language of the Revolution. Along with my other good friends, the young accordion and double bass player, the violinist was the last musician to join the Youth Communist Members.

Honour was so important to us, to our families, that we were always afraid of losing it. If girls and boys in the ensemble were seen talking, for example, late in the evening, after lights were out, then they would be severely and openly criticised. And so we learned to keep our feelings hidden, never to be obvious. I knew how proud my mother was of my position in the army ensemble and how she was honoured in the alleys because of this. At the beginning of the Spring Festival and on 1 August, the festival marking the founding

With my mother, in our courtyard

of Mao's Red Army, the street committee which represented our network of alleys used to send a special group marching through the *hutongs* playing red drums and cymbals, to honour the families of army members. They would march into our courtyard to give my mother presents of sunflower seeds, peanuts, fruit and pork and, as they shook her hand, I knew how proud she was.

Our headquarters controlled a large army division comprising a few thousand soldiers, some based in army hospitals in different parts of China, others based in the mountains where many of the supplies were stored. Mostly they were peasant boys, who could neither read nor write, their positions replaced in the countryside by city boys such as my friends Ai Tie Wan and Zhu Hong who, instead of learning to fight, were learning to grow rice and wheat. Our work as musicians, singers and dancers was to entertain these soldiers, to keep their spirits high and their belief in communism intact. I remember one occasion when we travelled to perform in the mountains, with our costumes and instruments beside us in the green army trucks. Ahead of us had gone a group of ten boys, to set up the wooden stage and lighting; this was hard work and to volunteer was considered to be a good communist gesture. As we drove into the brick army compound, the soldiers saluted us and we returned with 'back-salutes'.

Before the performance we sat together, boys and girls, applying our stage make-up: foundation to make our faces smooth under the lights, rouge to emphasise our cheekbones, a brush to paint our eyebrows 'like swords', black eyeliner to dramatise our eyes, dark red paint for our lips and powder to set the make-up. The wind instrumentalists, including myself, used to think this stage powder was bad for our breathing! While we worked on our faces, we talked about life. I remember liking one of the dancers and watching her painting her eyebrows and lips in the mirror, as she giggled with the other girls. But I never told her that I liked her. I cared too

much for my honour to show anything more than the subtlest kind of love. I don't think she ever guessed my feelings.
With the other dancers, she used to walk into the village to
buy chocolate. We were each paid seven *yuan* a month,
dancers, singers and musicians alike but, apart from buying
cigarettes, I used to keep these *yuan* to give to my mother
whenever I went home to the alleys, which was usually once a
month or once in two months. She used to take it quickly
from my hand and put it under the pillow on her wooden bed,
as though someone were about to take it from her: it was a
sudden gesture that always made me feel sad.

In the mountain compound, soldiers cooked us the best
food, in huge woks, four or five dishes at a time: dumplings
filled with pork and Chinese leaf, fried *dou-fu* with pork and
bai-cai, red stewed beef and stewed beef with potato. We were
treated very well. We were also asked to perform for the peasants in the nearby village, who felt that it was a great honour
to be entertained by musicians in this way. I played many of
the melodies on my bamboo flutes, accompanied by the
orchestra, as the girls performed their dances, always with a
revolutionary message. One such dance, I remember, was
about Tibet, and it had a beautiful introduction on the
bamboo flutes. The girls were dressed in brightly coloured
Tibetan costumes and the story was about a group of Tibetan
girls who wanted to wash the clothes of a Chinese *ban zhang*,
a soldier in charge of seven other soldiers. The soldier would
not let them wash his clothes, so they sang a song about why
they wanted to do this for a communist soldier. 'Who liber-
ated us?' the girls sang. 'Who saved us? The Liberation Army!'
The choreography, which included traditional Tibetan-style
dancing, the colourful costumes and the music were spectac-
ular, and the peasants watching the performance loved it.

Afterwards, to celebrate, I remember one of the peasant
farmers inviting four or five of us, all instrumentalists, into
his house to drink strong traditional wine, made from fer-

mented sorghum wheat, out of little porcelain cups. This colourless wine is even stronger than Russian vodka and I remember my friend the violinist getting very drunk. At the time, I was happy to play for people who so obviously appreciated what we were doing; as young musicians, we never thought beyond that and the pleasure of performing on stage. It is only now that I realise what my troop leader had meant when he handed me the box of flutes: such theatre was a powerful tool in communicating and promoting the ideas of communism, and its misrepresentation of reality. I knew very little about Tibet, apart from the stories that Xuan had told me about the minority singers and dancers in her company. I had no means of knowing the truth.

Still, from time to time, we had to work like peasants in the countryside and, for the first time, I worked alongside my musician friends in the rice fields. We stood barefoot together in water which came almost up to our knees, bending over and thrusting the green rice seedlings into the mud. These were thrown in bunches into the water, for us

Myself (second left, top row) with some of the musicians and dancers from my army ensemble, including the violinist (far left, bottom row) and the erhu player (far left, top row)

to separate and plant. We used to sing a song about planting the rice, competing with one another to see who was
the fastest and could plant in the straightest line. It was
hard, back-breaking work and I remember leeches clinging
to my legs beneath the water. If you felt one on your leg,
you had to give it an immediate, powerful slap to make it
fall off, before it could begin to take your blood.

Chapter 31

LOVE AND FRIENDSHIP: THE END OF THE REVOLUTION

In 1976, one week before my eighteenth birthday, Mao Zedong died. It's strange: I don't remember where I was when I heard the news, or what I was doing; I don't remember crying as we were all supposed to do. For ten years of my childhood, I had studied Mao's thoughts and poetry, looked on his image everywhere, performed songs, music and dances in his name, held *The Little Red Book* against my heart, worked in the rice and wheat fields for him, and been separated from my mother when I needed her most, because of him. As a musical child, I liked the artistic side of the Revolution: together with food and nature, the rhythms, movements and melodies of the Revolution were the things that made me feel happy as a child, and still do when I recall them. But I didn't care about the politics. In the end I was simply bored with Mao, an old man whose thoughts had taken up so much of my childhood. I knew I could have learned so many other things.

When Deng Xiaoping came to power in 1977, life in China slowly began to change. The idea of open, personal love, not just revolutionary love, was once again permitted in the alleys of Beijing; and a wedding was now a lively, traditional, colour-ful affair, so different to my sister Kai's revolutionary marriage. People were free to celebrate their love with a tradi-tional combination of good food, strong rice wine and at least a hundred bicycles converging on a single courtyard. Couples were married in the local registry office, where papers were signed, but the festivities always took place at home. When I was 19, and still a musician in the army ensemble, I attended the marriage celebrations of a singer in my brother Yi's company, the Beijing Film Orchestra, which employed many musicians, singers and composers. My brother's friend, who had a very good tenor voice, was marrying a girl who worked in a factory which made material for clothes. I think they were really in love.

It was a very hot summer and the family had brought their stove outside, into the courtyard, to make *rou me mian* (minced meat noodles), a special dish of handmade noodles with minced pork, spring onion, soy sauce and sliced cucum-ber. This is a famous dish in Beijing, one that I had often cooked alongside the *suona* player in my own courtyard and of course a symbolic one, representing long life and a happy marriage. The noodles were prepared in a vast wok and the family had borrowed many porcelain bowls and bamboo chopsticks from their neighbours, in preparation for the feast. There was a lot of traditional singing and drinking of rice wine and beer but the bride herself, dressed in a red tra-ditional jacket and light-coloured trousers, was shy and formal as the celebrations began. There is a rule, however, at Chinese weddings, that the bride and groom must drink a toast with every guest: this meant saying *'Gan-bei!'* perhaps a hundred times, emptying a tiny porcelain cup filled with very strong rice wine each time, and smacking your lips to show that you have finished your wine and that it was deli-cious. In those days, women were not used to drinking rice wine, or even beer, and I remember the bride getting a little bit drunk in the end, after celebrating with so many friends from the Film Orchestra and neighbours from the alleys.

In Beijing at that time, drinking games were popular among men and always played a part in courtyard celebrations. These loud games are a curious mixture of poetry, mathematics and rice wine, a theatre of hand movements, rhythmic sentences and numbers exchanged at high speed, until players are standing on their chairs with excitement. Among the traditional musicians and singers of my childhood, the rhythms and rhymes had an added sense of musical theatre, the different tones of the language dramatising the game. For example, a player might begin with the line *'Ge liang hao ya'* (we are two brothers), putting his right thumb out in front of him. At the same time, the other player might put out three fingers. If the total number of fingers equals the number spoken in the sentence, the player who has spoken the line has to empty his cup of rice wine. The second player might then say the line *'Ba pi ma ya'* (eight horses), putting out three fingers. If the first player has put out five fingers, then his friend, who spoke the line, has to drink his cup of rice wine. The sentences must rhyme and are often very poetic.

China was beginning to open a little, relaxing some of the extraordinary rules that had come to be accepted as normality. For example, when I was 16, 17, if a boy saw a pretty girl walking down the street and approached her, simply to talk, he could be arrested and beaten for having 'bad thoughts'. The only time we could really be with girls, talking openly, was on our skating expeditions to the Summer Palace. But in 1978 we were given the chance to meet and be close to girls in public for the first time, at dances which were known as Jiao Ji Wu (literally meaning 'make friend dance'). Every two or three weeks I would return to Beijing from my travels with the army ensemble, dressed in my army-green uniform, with the big padded coat and fur hat in the winter. The dances were held in schools and universities, where normal studies had finally resumed, on the premises of companies and in the cinemas and theatres of Beijing. We danced waltzes to the music of Strauss and the tango, either to Western music or to traditional Chinese melodies. There were usually two bands: one comprising a saxophone, accordion, trombone, clarinet and other brass or woodwind instruments; the other all traditional Chinese instruments, the *erhu*, *sheng*, *pipa* and bamboo flutes. The girls, many with long black hair worn loose again for the first time since the Cultural Revolution, danced in long colourful skirts or trousers with patterned blouses. Still, we were not allowed to hold them too close, or dance too slowly.

But after the dance, we would make appointments to meet again, in Bei-hai Park or in the gardens of the Summer Palace. Arriving on bicycles, we would sit in a restaurant at a little round wooden table, drinking jasmine tea and eating together. Favourite dishes were steamed rice with *hong shao dou-fu* (red stewed bean curd), *hong shao qie-zi* (red stewed aubergine with pork) or *mian bao* (flour parcel) and *jia xiang chang* (perfumed sausage). *Mian bao*, similar to the steamed *man-tou* buns of my early childhood, were thought to be more fashionable, like Western white rolls, because they were puffy and light, without the sticky texture of *man-tou*. The round slices of pork sausage were very good because they had a pure, meat taste. We drank our tea from porcelain cups and then walked, holding hands, talking about music, poetry, nature. In the Summer Palace, we would go to the river and sit on the rocks, near a Buddhist temple that had been vandalised by the Red Guards during the Cultural Revolution. As far as a man's arm could reach with a hammer, the heads of Buddha figures had been smashed and broken but, above that height, they remained intact. We would set a tape recorder down on one of the rocks and play music while we danced.

After the public dances had finished, at around 11 o'clock in the evening, my friends and I would ride our bicycles home towards the alleys. Five hours of energetic dancing had made us ravenously hungry and we were always full of good humour, wanting to talk about who we had met and who we were going to see again. On the way home we used to pass a very little, cheap, traditional restaurant. In China, when we describe a restaurant as being 'cheap', this usually means good: such places are small and simple, without any pretension, but the food is delicious, like the best home cooking, with really fresh ingredients. In this particular restaurant, with its bare wooden tables and chairs, and dark interior, I would sit with three or four friends at a corner table and order the best food to share while we talked. We would begin with a couple of starters, *tou-pan*, dishes known in Beijing as *liang-cai*. One of our favourites was cold seaweed served with chopped garlic and a drizzle of sesame seed oil on the top. This seaweed, which is bought dried, has to be soaked and washed many times over to remove all the salt. Another delicious starter would be *hai zhe ban huang gua* (meaning 'sea plant table-cooked cucumber'), which has a tasty, chewy sea texture. With these dishes we would each have a large glass of Beijing beer.

By that time of night it was too late to order any fried dishes but we could still have *hun-tun* soup, which we loved. This was cooked on a big coal stove in the restaurant itself, so we could see the two or three cooks preparing it. They used a huge, thick metal wok, at least one metre in diameter. The stock which they used for the soup was fantastic because so many meat bones had been boiled for many hours in the wok, until the water had turned a whitish-creamy colour, and the flavour of the meat stock was deep and strong. Together we would order two big bowls of *hun-tun* soup, each bowl being four times bigger than a normal bowl, with at least 12 to 15 'parcels' in each one. We could see them putting the *hun-tun* into the wok of meaty soup while we talked and then in only a few minutes they were ready to eat. First, some chopped spring onion and fresh green coriander were put into the bottom of each bowl, with tiny dried shrimp skins which add an amazing flavour,

In my winter army uniform with Liu Qing Puo

followed by some soy sauce, sesame seed oil and a little bit of chilli oil. Then the *hun-tun* soup itself was ladled into each bowl, and at that moment, as all the flavours combined, the smell would be incredible, especially during the winter when all the windows were steamed up and it was cold outside. This simple restaurant was always crowded with people though, and sometimes we would have to wait in a queue outside, singing Russian or revolutionary songs to keep our minds off our hunger. Sometimes, even after waiting, there would be no space inside and then we would stand on the pavement outside to eat our food, talking and afterwards always smoking. It would be one o'clock in the morning by the time I arrived home in my courtyard, letting myself in quietly so as not to wake my mother.

RECIPES

- *Hong shao dou-fu* (red stewed bean curd) with pork
  see pages 215–17
- *Quing zheng wan-zi* (steamed pork and prawn balls)
  see pages 217–19

Chapter 32

I AM A MUSICIAN

Music, singing and dancing had played such an important part in the Revolution; but China was now changing, the Revolution was over and we were no longer needed. One morning in 1979, after weeks of rumours that had spread through the theatre and practice rooms of the compound, we were summoned to the meeting room, singers, dancers, instrumentalists together. 'I am so sorry for all of you,' the troop leader began. 'There is a new government policy regarding small army music companies: you are all dismissed as artists. From tomorrow, you will be given new orders and you will change your professions. We will decide what you are going to do.' Some of the girls, who were such talented dancers, with many years of training and dreams behind them, burst into tears; others went immediately to the troop leader to talk to him about working in Beijing, close to their homes, as nurses in the army hospital. 'We will speak to you all individually,' he replied. 'We will decide where you go.'

Many of the dancers were sent to be trained as nurses in army hospitals, some as they had hoped in Beijing, others in towns such as Tianjin and Baoding; some were even sent as far as Mongolia. Once again, we had no control over our lives. 'Guo Yue, you are to go to the little town of Yi Xian in the Hebei Province to train as a soldier. You have one day to go home and prepare. You are now dismissed. You are no longer a musician.' I had to hand over my flutes.

I travelled by train with two of my friends, a singer called Dai Heng Ming (meaning 'forever bright'), who was going to work as a mechanic on the army trucks, and an actor, Zhao Da Ming (big and bright), who was tall, good looking, from an educated family and talented at reciting poetry. He was very left-wing in his political beliefs and was the only artist among the new performers, or *xing bing* (new soldiers) as we were known in the ensemble, to have been successful in becoming a Communist Party member. He had asked to be given a gun and to become a soldier straight away: this was an honourable gesture and he was placed in the first division. I was going into the seventh division, so we were separated.

When I arrived in the army compound, in a landscape that was just bare, yellow earth with small mountains and no trees, I was taken by a *ban zhang* (group leader) to the barracks where I was to share a room with seven other soldiers, including the leader himself. 'Guo Yue!' he said in his countryside dialect, 'this is your bed.' I stood there in front of these seven soldiers, all boys from the countryside, who had never been educated, who couldn't read or write. I couldn't relate to them; I felt I couldn't even talk to them. Apart from the beds, made like *dou-fu*, there was a wooden stand in the room supporting six big guns, each with a bayonet that could be folded down, and one semi-automatic rifle. The group leader, who was in charge of the others, explained: 'We will apply for a gun for you.' I couldn't believe that a gun was now going to replace my bamboo flutes. I felt like a frog who had jumped into the wrong pond. I would have preferred to become a peasant farmer working in the fields. 'I am a musician,' I said, trying to steady my voice. 'Isn't there anything else that I can do for the army? Isn't there any way that I can use my music to help these soldiers?' The group leader looked surprised and then after a moment's thought replied, 'I will speak to the *lian zhang*,' his superior. Later, I was summoned to see this leader. 'So you are a musician. Very good. You can be the musical director and conductor of all our *ban* groups. You must get them to sing as they march and we will see which group can sing the loudest.'

The next day, as the soldiers marched, I stood before them, teaching them a song line by line, with a lot of good rhythms for marching:

> *The sun is going down.*
> *We went to practise shooting.*
> *We are singing beautiful, bright songs.*
> *We are happy with what we do.*

There were hundreds of soldiers and I was the only one walking outside their lines, not carrying a gun. 'Guo Yue!' I was commanded. 'It is now time for the *ge yong bi sai* (singing competition).' I divided the soldiers into groups of 200 and directed them to sing in parts, with one group following another, to see which section could sing the loudest. That group would then receive the highest praise. The young soldiers sat crosslegged on the ground, their guns resting on their shoulders and I could see how much they enjoyed the singing. Preparing the songs, conducting the soldiers, this was my new work and I was happy up to a point. I was still involved with music, though on these basic terms, but I was lonely. I didn't understand many of the soldiers' dialects; some had come from as far as the Yunnan Province in the south of China and, in not taking up a gun, I could not become one of them. I knew that, from time to time, one of the soldiers would ask their group leader, 'Why doesn't Guo

Yue have to be a normal soldier?' 'We want to use his musical training,' was the reply they were given, but I'm sure they must have continued to question this in their minds.

The only time I really felt that I was accepted as one of them was when we all made *jiaozi* together. Ten soldiers were ordered to make a stuffing for the dumplings in a huge army wok, chopping the pork and *bai-cai* very finely and combining these with chopped ginger and spring onion. Other soldiers made a vast amount of dough which was then measured out by weight, for each *ban* of eight soldiers to collect, together with a measured amount of stuffing. We then took this back to our rooms, to make the dumplings together. The soldiers in my group, young men of 17, 18, could each eat as many as 50 dumplings, so our *ban* alone had to make 400 dumplings. After we had rolled the dough and formed the *jiaozi* into their traditional folds, we took them back to the army kitchen, where they were boiled and put into a big metal basin. We had to stand in a queue, to wait our turn. Then, taking our dumplings outside, we squatted on the ground to eat them, putting some soy sauce and vinegar into our individual metal bowls and picking up the dumplings with plain bamboo chopsticks. It was a good feeling, eating outside with the soldiers, beneath the sky.

After one year as musical director, I was allowed to go home to Beijing. I became a freelance flute player, performing for traditional opera companies and other music companies, playing my own small collection of bamboo flutes. I no longer had a silver flute. I was happy to be in the alleys again, cooking for my mother, dancing and eating with my friends, meeting girls. But inside I was restless: like my mother in Harbin, I wanted to see the world. The alleys felt so poor, so narrow: there was no space to breathe. You never knew how far you could go, before you had stepped over the line.

In 1981 my third sister Yan, the most modern and adventurous of all my sisters, went with some friends to Huang

*With my brother Yi and two
friends beside the river in Beijing
where I played as a little boy*

Shan (Yellow Mountain) in the Anhui Province. Walking up behind her was a young Frenchman, who was travelling by himself in China, trying to learn the language. By the time he reached the top of the mountain, he had met my sister, and they walked down together, falling in love. It was not easy to have a relationship with a foreigner at that time, but my sister is a determined character and she married him, leaving China for London, where he was to teach at the Lycée Français school, in Kensington. Once in London, Yan heard about the Guildhall School of Music and Drama and applied to the British Embassy in Beijing for her youngest brother to further his studies of the silver flute. The Chinese government gave their permission for me to leave and I received a passport which was more than gold to me. China was so vast but the spirit of the people was so suppressed by communism that it felt small. I wanted to be free.

Chapter 33

THE END OF MY CHILDHOOD

My last day in Beijing, in May 1982, was celebrated with a great feast of *jiaozi*: hundreds of dumplings made by my family and friends. Twenty people in all, mostly singers, musicians and dancers from my army ensemble, we sat on the steps inside my courtyard and on wooden stools, around the little worn-out table (*xiao zhuo*) that my father had made when I was small. My sisters were rolling the dough into circles, the rhythm of their hands as continuous as their conversation, while my friends and I filled these circles with a mixture of minced pork, chopped *xi hu-lu* (squash), egg and ginger, folding and sealing each dumpling with unthinking dexterity, while we talked and talked for hours. We also made a *tou-pan* dish of glass noodles (*liang ban fen-si*), symbolising long life – a tradition when friends are parting. There was a lot of laughter and singing but also a sadness that filled the courtyard. It was exciting, to be entering the unknown, travelling towards a freedom that in my heart I longed for. But to do so meant leaving the people I loved, most of all my mother.

After I had left for London, via Hong Kong, my father's

sister travelled from the Henan Province to stay with my family. I had never met her but my sisters sent me a letter about her visit. She had bound feet but was very tall, like my father, and was very traditional. She loved food and Chinese rice wine, drinking one bottle a day. My sisters told me how angry she was with my mother, for allowing me to leave China: 'Guo Yue is the roots of the Guo family,' she said. 'Now the roots of the grass have gone.' My mother didn't answer. But as I read this letter, I remembered an old Chinese poem that my mother had often recited to me when I was a little boy:

> *The spring silkworm*
> *makes the silk*
> *until there is no more silk to give.*
> *A candle, when it is burning,*
> *has already ash and tears dripping down.*
> *All the time it gives light*
> *until itself is finished.*

With my mother

167

I knew, however much my mother wanted me to stay, that she was the most determined to let me go. 'In the end,' she used to say, 'the little bird must fly. It can't be always hiding beneath its mother's wing.'

RECIPE

• *Liang ban fen-si* (cold mixed silk noodles) *see pages* 187–9

Chapter 34

RETURNING TO THE HUTONGS

My mother died in October 1994, after years of being unable to move, unable to talk. When I saw her, finally free, she looked so beautiful and calm. After a little while, my sisters buried her ashes as she had wanted, in the earth beneath some green bamboo, which now bends in the wind, making its natural music.

In December 1994, I returned to Beijing with Clare, who was to become my wife. I wanted to show her the alleys where I had spent my childhood, the vegetable markets where tomatoes and aubergines were heaped like treasure, the ice on the lakes of the Summer Palace, the Drum Tower surrounded by stalls selling noodles, red-bean buns and thousand-year eggs, and my mother's flat, which was always full of sunshine, where she had spent the last ten years of her life. As we sat in this room with my sister Kai, drinking jasmine tea and eating sunflower seeds, while Liu Qing Puo mopped the floor where we had walked in snow from outside, I remembered my sisters telling me how my mother had clung to a wooden stool in the outer room of our courtyard home, not wanting to leave the alleys.

The following day, we took a yellow taxi to the *hutongs*, stopping outside a shop that used to be the grocery shop where I had bought vegetables as a child. Walking the few steps up the alley, we looked through the entrance to my courtyard: leaning against what had once been the *suona* player's little brick kitchen was an old sweeping brush. I longed to go in and push open the door of our outer room. Somehow I could still hear my sisters' laughter and the songs they used to sing. I could hear my mother's voice brightening: 'Xiao Yue! What shall we eat today?' 'Let's walk a bit,' I said. Around the corner, in a neighbouring alley, a man in blue-padded cotton jacket and trousers was selling vegetables and pickles in metal basins and red plastic buckets. The bright winter sunshine cast shadows of bare trees on to the brick wall of the alley, where he had nailed his calendar. On another wall, written in white chalk, was a line of government propaganda: 'Having one child is good. Having two children is not good.'

In the shadows of the early morning, we went to the ghost market in Beijing, where people from the countryside set out newspaper on the ground each week, to sell old things, from textiles to bird cages. Stamping her feet to keep warm, Clare found an old lacquer jewellery box covered with layers of dust: underneath were flowers, butterflies and fish painted on the outside, opening to reveal secret drawers and boxes, with a mirror bordered in red-painted wood. 'My mother would have liked this,' I said, remembering how, when she could still communicate a little, she had asked my sisters to find her a lipstick. She still wanted to look beautiful.

It seemed that every other person we met in Beijing was a property developer, a restaurant owner, an antiques dealer or a business entrepreneur, including my old friend the violinist from my army ensemble who now had his own furniture factory. 'There is no money in music, Guo Yue,' he said. 'I know an artist you can still meet,' Kai said one afternoon and so it was that we went to visit Zhao Jia Xi (Happy Home), the calligrapher who had sung in the fields with Liang. He lived in two rooms on the third floor of a modern apartment block. Everywhere you looked there were piles of books, on shelves, stacked up on the floor, beside pots of calligraphy brushes, ink stones and sheets of rice paper. Handing us glasses of hot jasmine tea, he asked us how we had met and said that he would do a piece of calligraphy for us, bringing together literature and music. Having prepared the ink, he draped a large sheet of rice paper, arranging our hands and positions so that the paper had only air underneath, but still would not move as he worked. Then, after a few minutes of silent thought, he wrote a poem, moving his brush between us like a dancer over the paper. It was a beautiful performance, like an improvised melody, controlled and yet free.

He explained that the characters could be read in two different ways: horizontally, from left to right, or as two vertical lines. Beside the poem he wrote, 'Guo Yue and Clare, for you'.

Bamboo	Tea
Rain	Smoke
Pine	Tree
Wind	Moon
Music	Books
Rhythms	Sound

'Your home is far too messy, Zhao Jia Xi!' my sister reprimanded him. 'You should tidy up! I don't know why you never found yourself a wife.' We waited for the ink to dry and then he rolled the calligraphy for us, explaining that we would have to have it mounted on stronger paper when we got home. We said our goodbyes and thanks and left this charming man. Clare always remembers how moved she was when, as we walked to the door, she glanced into his bedroom. On the wall beside his bed was a poster of Marilyn Monroe, her white dress lifted by the wind. 'I have never met anyone so talented, or so lonely,' she said.

I couldn't show her the clear water of the river, the willow trees or the dragonflies. Concrete has replaced the dark banks of earth and new trees have been installed in systematic lines. All around, as far as the eye can see, modern apartment blocks are soaring into the sky. In big hotels, string quartets play the music of Mozart and Vivaldi as people drink coffee and talk business. The remnants of my childhood are fast disappearing.

On one of our last days in Beijing, we sat in the restaurant of the Summer Palace, drinking jasmine tea and eating hot sultana cake. On the walls were murals of the English countryside. Outside, in the clear sunshine, we walked hand in hand beside the frozen lake where I had skated with my friends 20 years before, to the rocks where we had sat together to eat our food, reciting poetry, singing revolutionary songs and talking about the lives we wanted to lead. Since then I have experienced freedom, and I value that. But still, there is a part of me that has remained in the *hutongs*, amid the colours, smells, rhythms and sounds of my childhood world. And it is that part that comes alive again, each time I begin to prepare the ingredients and cook in my London kitchen, or practise my long notes and traditional melodies on the bamboo flutes. Although it is now more than 20 years since the courtyard feast that marked the end of my childhood, the traditions that I brought with me from China, the music and cooking that I learned in my courtyard home, have kept my childhood vivid, in both my imagination and senses. Food, like music, is evocative to an almost magical degree.

I hope this magic will also work for you, when you make the dishes we have written down in this book. I hope, through the colours, textures, sounds and flavours of Chinese home cooking, that you will gain a special insight, a sensual impression if you like, of a musical childhood in Beijing before, during and after the Cultural Revolution.

RECIPES

- Sesame prawns on toast *see pages* 189–90
- Trout with coriander *see pages* 231–2
- Seafood *tang mian* (noodle soup) with scallops, prawns, squid and handmade noodles *see pages* 247–9
- Prawns and (green flower) broccoli *see pages* 230–1

Part Two

·

RECIPES

A note on ingredients

In this book I want to give you the chance to create authentic Chinese home cooking. I have, however, made a few adjustments to traditional recipes, incorporating certain ingredients that were not available in my childhood, and taking both taste and health into account.

For example, when I was little we mainly used the highly rationed peanut oil and a little animal fat, or lard. Now I like to use sunflower oil in my cooking: it is lighter, good for you, and you are never too conscious of its presence in a dish. I also tend to use sea salt in my dishes now, rather than the traditional rock salt, though you might like to try both and come to your own decision. I would also say that in traditional Chinese home cooking a lot of fatty meat is eaten; for example, when you are cooking red stewed pork, it is traditionally thought that using a lot of pork fat improves the taste. Now I would suggest using organic pork for the taste, but not using too much fat.

To ensure that your dishes have the best taste and are good for your body, I would recommend that you buy organic *doufu* (fresh bean curd) if possible, from a good source. (You will find that in the West it is usually written as 'tofu', which comes from the Cantonese word for bean curd, rather than the Mandarin.) Equally important is always to choose a good soy sauce, one that has been made using a natural fermentation process. I must also say that in recipes requiring a light vinegar as one of the key flavouring notes, I now often prefer to use Western white wine vinegar in place of Chinese white rice vinegar, which doesn't have the same quality of taste that I remember from my childhood. But again I recommend that you try both and make your own choice.

To give you a taste of how the traditional cooking techniques and approaches which I learned in my courtyard can be applied and adapted to certain vegetables – and especially

177

to fish and certain seafoods – that were not available to me in my childhood, I am also including a few modern recipes, which are favourites in my family.

To buy the authentic dried and preserved ingredients (lily-flower, bamboo shoots, Chinese wood-ear) and to get some idea of the wonderful diversity of Chinese vegetables, you will need to visit a specialist Chinese food shop. Keep an open mind before you go, and in your choice of vegetables allow yourself to be spontaneous: look for the most beautiful, fresh colours and make sure you touch and smell each one that tempts your eye before you make your choice. I would recommend you do the same in your local supermarket or farmers' market, where you will find a lot of the ingredients for Chinese home cooking. If you buy good, fresh ingredients, you are well on the way to creating delicious food.

I am assuming, in my recipes, that you will wash all your vegetables carefully before preparing them. Because the cooking process is often quite fast, like a sequence of steps in a dance, it's also a good idea to read the whole recipe through carefully before you start, and to have all your ingredients measured out and prepared, ready to be used at the right time.

A note on chopping

To work on your chopping technique, bend the knuckles on both the index and third fingers of your left hand (or your right if you are left-handed) so that, when you're resting the tips of those fingers on your work surface, they look like kneeling figures. The knife can then lean against the vertical wall created by your fingers, and can move up and down very fast. If you follow this technique correctly you will not cut yourself, but do begin by chopping slowly – and practise! Try to use a heavier knife to give your chopping a good rhythm.

Your store cupboard and essential equipment for Chinese home cooking

There are certain ingredients which you should always have to hand, the key ingredients for Chinese home cooking: white rice, plain and self-raising white flour, dark and light soy sauce (without artificial colouring or flavourings), sunflower oil, Chinese white rice vinegar (or you can use Western white wine vinegar as a good alternative) and dark rice vinegar (I buy Chinkiang rice vinegar, which is similar in taste to Italian balsamic vinegar), Chinese cooking rice wine (I recommend Shaoxing rice wine), sesame seed oil, white caster sugar, cornflour, sea salt, rock salt, white pepper, black pepper, star anise, Sichuan peppercorns, chilli oil, chilli sauce, dried lily-flower, dried Chinese wood-ear, dried mushroom, dried chilli, ginger, garlic, sesame seed paste, raw shelled peanuts, dried shrimps, dried flour noodles, dried green bean thread or glass noodles (*fen-si*) and sesame seeds. With these in your store cupboard, you are ready for most recipes! You can then be spontaneous, if you like, when choosing your fresh ingredients.

I would also recommend that you have the following simple equipment: a big wooden chopping board, a good wok, a medium-size bamboo steamer, a colander, a wooden spatula and spoon, a wire scoop with a wooden handle (or the modern equivalent) for taking dumplings or noodles out of boiling water, a good heavy knife (you don't have to use a Chinese chopper, but a weighty knife will give you a good rhythm and prevent you from chopping your fingers), and bamboo chopsticks, for cooking as well as eating.

Planning a feast

The quantities I have given in my recipes are for dishes that will happily serve four to six people. For this number of guests, I recommend that you serve a couple of starters, followed by four to six hot dishes – for example, one fish, one meat and a few vegetable dishes, including those with egg and *dou-fu* (bean curd). The tradition is to end with a light soup.

Remember, however, that noodle soup and *hun-tun* soup are substantial dishes in their own right, often accompanied by steamed *man-tou* for lunch, or a couple of very tasty dishes for dinner. The ancient, symbolic *jiaozi* (dumplings) are served by themselves, with a special sauce. The complex ritual of making them, which demands time, patience and practice, is as much a part of the family celebration, as much an expression of love, as the feast itself.

For the end of your meal, I suggest that you serve cold watermelon or big fresh oranges, together with Chinese tea, to cleanse your palate.

In China we have an old saying:

> *Fan yao che hao,*
> *jiao yao shui hao,*
> *lu yao zou hao.*

(Eat well, sleep well, walk well, and you will live to be over one hundred.)

To this good advice I would add a little of my own: drink good wine, listen to beautiful music, enjoy your cooking with family and friends, and you will enjoy your life!

STARTERS
Tou-pan (head-plate) dishes

These light, exquisite dishes were an imagined luxury in my early childhood. My mother used to tell us how, when she was a girl in Harbin, her family would have many starters, like a beautiful prelude, before the sequence of main dishes commenced. I used to watch the black and white films that were made about life in China during the 1930s, before Mao, delighting in the long silk traditional clothes, and conjuring up in my mind a whole assortment of delicious starters.

Egg, Potato and Beansprouts

Combining crunchy textures with shades of pale gold and vibrant green, this simple dish has all the qualities of a musical prelude. The Sichuan pepper, one of the spices much loved by the Chinese, is optional; it will give a dynamic edge to what is otherwise a very natural, pure and tasty dish. Beautiful to eat on a summer's evening, in the faded heat of our courtyard.

INGREDIENTS

1 x 250 g (9 oz) packet of beansprouts
sea salt
1 large white potato, peeled and cut into very thin sticks, the same size as the beansprouts – do this by slicing the potato very finely into rounds, piling up a few of these at a time and slicing into fine stick-shapes
2 eggs, well beaten

ingredients continue ➤

2 spring onions, washed and chopped separately – divide each
    one in half lengthwise and then finely chop, including the
    green section which will provide the intense colour in this dish
sunflower oil
1 clove of garlic, peeled and finely chopped
Chinese white rice vinegar (or Western white wine vinegar)
light soy sauce
Sichuan peppercorns (the reddish brown dried berries of the
    prickly ash tree)
sesame seed oil

METHOD

Begin by bringing a pan of water to the boil, and adding the
beansprouts. After 5 minutes, drain them through a colander,
adding a pinch of salt. Then prepare another pan of boiling
water for the potato, which will take only 1–2 minutes to cook,
depending on how fine your stick-shapes are; the potato
should be cooked but very crunchy, the colour a beautiful
pale yellow. When the beansprouts have cooled a little, gently
squeeze out the excess water with your hands – but be careful
not to make them too dry. Put them into a dish and taste one;
it should still be crunchy, with a light, fresh taste. Now add
the potato to the same dish.

    In a bowl, add 2 pinches of salt to the beaten eggs and one
of the finely chopped spring onions. You are now going to
make Chinese 'crispy fried egg'. Heat your wok on a medium-
high heat until it is hot, then add 2 tablespoons of sunflower
oil. Heat the oil until it is just smoking: if you bend down to
the level of the wok, you can clearly see when the smoke is just
beginning to rise from the oil. At this point, add the second
finely chopped spring onion; this should make a good sound,
like cymbals. When the sound has faded, after about 15
seconds, add the egg – there will be another percussive sound
if your heat is correct – and move it around swiftly with a

wooden spoon or spatula until it turns a golden, crispy brown. Add this mixture to the dish containing the beansprouts and potato, followed by the finely chopped garlic. Over all these ingredients pour evenly 1 dessertspoon of white rice vinegar (or Western white wine vinegar) and 2½ dessertspoons of light soy sauce.

Heat a small, strong saucepan over a medium-high heat. When it is hot, add 2 tablespoons of oil, and continue to heat until the oil is really smoking. At this point, if you wish, you can add 10–20 Sichuan peppercorns; in the hot oil, within a few seconds, they will turn completely black. Now, holding the saucepan at arm's length (because the oil can spit), pour the hot oil over the beansprouts, potato, egg and garlic; it will make a really dramatic sound. If you are using Sichuan pepper, you can place a metal sieve over the dish to catch the peppercorns, leaving only the flavour or, as the Chinese prefer, you can simply include them in the final dish: when eaten black and crispy they will make your tongue feel pleasantly numb! Add a final drizzle of sesame seed oil and serve.

Hot Peanuts

We used to say that these hot peanuts, eaten outside in the courtyard with light Beijing beer, were the most delicious things. An essential starter in the *hutong*s.

INGREDIENTS

sunflower oil
4 handfuls of raw shelled peanuts – you can buy good ones
    in a specialist Chinese shop, or of course in any
    Western supermarket
sea salt or rock salt

METHOD

Heat the wok on a medium-high heat, and when it's hot add 2 tablespoons of oil. Put the peanuts into the wok and stir, turning the heat down to medium-low. Move the nuts around all the time and ensure that they are all coated with oil, then stir gently from side to side – we say like weaving silk. They will be ready in 3 minutes. Place in a serving bowl, leaving the oil in the wok for another dish; the peanuts won't have used it up. Sprinkle on some salt – you should hear a good sizzling sound, and the nuts will look glossy.

Liang ban qin-cai si

COLD MIXED CELERY SILK WITH *DOU-FU* (BEAN CURD) AND EGG

This cold dish demonstrates the approach to colour and texture in Chinese home cooking. It is light, refreshing and full of nutrition, with subtle colours that conceal a surprising depth of taste. In China, celery is thought to be very good for your blood pressure. This idea, that a dish is both delicious and healthy, is central to our thinking on food.

INGREDIENTS

1 bunch of (preferably organic) celery, thoroughly washed
sunflower oil
1 pack of fresh *dou-fu* (bean curd)
2 eggs
sea salt
1 spring onion, washed and finely chopped
white caster sugar
light soy sauce

Chinese white rice vinegar (or Western white wine vinegar)
sesame seed oil
sesame seeds

METHOD

Begin by preparing the celery. After washing it, take one stick at a time and break it in half, pulling the strings down as you do so and removing them. There tend to be more strings on organic celery – they look as if you could play music on them! Bring a pan of water to the boil, add the celery and cook for 1½–2 minutes, until it turns a very intense, light to medium green. Removing any hard end pieces, cut into lengths of 6 cm (2½ in). Taking each piece, slice horizontally into one end of the celery, almost to the other end, but leaving it still attached. Slice two or three more fine layers in this way, so that they look like the pages of a book. Then, turning each piece lengthwise, slice very finely. In Chinese, we call this cutting technique 'shredding'. Leave to one side in a dish.

Now for the *dou-fu*. In China there are two kinds of fresh *dou-fu*: *nan dou-fu* (southern bean curd), which is very soft and delicate, and *bei dou-fu* (northern bean curd), which is firmer. For the recipes in this book you will need to use the latter, which you can find in most supermarkets (usually written as 'tofu', from the Cantonese). It generally comes in one large rectangular piece. Cut this in half and then into smaller brick shapes, about 5 cm (2 in) in length.

Heat the wok on a medium-high heat until it is hot, then add 3 tablespoons of sunflower oil. When the oil begins to smoke, put the *dou-fu* in; you will hear a good percussive sound. The *dou-fu*, a 'cold' ingredient we say, looks as if it is dancing in the bubbles of oil. Holding the wok in the air, move it around so that the *dou-fu* is evenly coated, then leave to cook on a high heat – moving the *dou-fu* occasionally to prevent sticking – for about 6–7 minutes, until one side is a toasted golden-brown. Turn the pieces over and cook the other side, which should take about 4 minutes. Remove from the wok using chopsticks, leaving the remaining oil in the wok. Allow the *dou-fu* to cool a little before cutting each piece lenthwise into about 8 strips; then add all these to your dish of green celery. You should find that the *dou-fu* is golden and crispy on the outside, with a softer, open, light texture inside. This is the beauty of *dou-fu*.

Break 2 eggs into a bowl and add a couple of pinches of salt. Now finely chop a spring onion, using both white and green parts, and put half into the bowl with the eggs. Chop the other half even more finely and sprinkle over the *dou-fu*. Whisk the eggs and spring onion together. Add another table-spoonful of oil to that remaining in your wok, and heat on a very high heat. Wait until the oil is smoking, then put in the egg and spring onion mixture; this should bubble immedi-ately in the hot oil. Move the egg around with your chopsticks and watch as it immediately begins to turn a golden-brown colour; keep moving the mixture around, in different direc-tions, until it is broken and crispy. Make sure you haven't left any of the egg mixture in the bowl.

Now put your crispy egg on to the *dou-fu*, spring onion and celery, and add the following: 1 teaspoon of caster sugar, 1 tablespoon of light soy sauce, 3 pinches of sea salt, and 1 tea-spoon of light vinegar. Mix all these ingredients together, in a larger dish if necessary. Finally, add a drizzle of sesame seed oil and a scattering of sesame seeds.

Liang ban fen-si

COLD MIXED SILK NOODLES

The symbolic starter that marked the end of my childhood. The noodles, which we call glass noodles because of their transparency, or silk noodles because of their texture when boiled, are green-bean or mung-bean threads which represent long life, and are a tradition at birthdays, marriages and leaving-feasts, served cold with jasmine tea or light Beijing beer. In China, when we part, we say '*Zai-jian*' (See you again), never goodbye.

INGREDIENTS

225 g (8 oz) *fen-si* (glass noodles, or 'green-bean thread')
sunflower oil
½ cucumber, peeled and cut in half lengthwise, then finely sliced lengthwise into very thin strips
6 very thin slices of peeled ginger, finely chopped
2 cloves of garlic, peeled, crushed and finely chopped
3 spring onions, washed and finely chopped (use both green and white parts)
125 g (4½ oz) pork (preferably organic), cut very, very finely, ideally by hand, or minced, and then tossed in a little cornflour
Chinese dark rice vinegar (I suggest Chinkiang vinegar)
light soy sauce
sea salt
Sichuan peppercorns (the reddish brown dried berries of the prickly ash tree)
1 small, fresh red chilli (optional), cut in half across the centre and then in half lengthwise, then cut diagonally into small strips
sesame seed oil
fresh coriander, finely chopped (optional)

METHOD

First, boil your glass noodles for 3–4 minutes until they are soft and silky. Keep stirring them with chopsticks while they are boiling, so that they don't stick together. Drain them using a colander and put into a serving dish. Add 2 tablespoons of sunflower oil and mix well into the noodles so that they develop a silvery sheen. Before you start you can cut them shorter with scissors if you like, to make them more manageable – but since they are a symbol of long life I like to keep mine as long as possible! Lay the very fine strips of cucumber on to the noodles.

Next prepare your pork. Heat the wok on a medium-high heat until it is hot, and add 2 tablespoons of sunflower oil. Allow the oil to get hot, but not so hot that it's smoking. First, add the ginger, garlic and spring onion; there should be a good percussive sound. After a minute, add the pork, stirring all the time. After another minute, add ½ tablespoon of light soy sauce, still stirring continuously until, after a further 1–2 minutes, the pork has browned and become slightly crispy. Add it to the noodles and cucumber in your dish. Then add the following: 1½ tablespoons of Chinese dark rice vinegar, 2 tablespoons of light soy sauce and 1 teaspoon of sea salt. Mix thoroughly together.

Now, take a small saucepan, turn your heat to high and heat the pan until it is hot. Add 2½ tablespoons of sunflower oil and heat until it is smoking a little. Put in ½ teaspoon of the reddish brown Sichuan pepper, and your fresh red chilli (optional), cut into small diagonal strips. In just over a minute the peppercorns should have turned a brown-black colour and gone crispy, while the red chilli will have become singed around the edges. Immediately pour the oil, chilli and pepper over the dish – there should be a loud sound like a clash of cymbals. Drizzle a very little sesame seed oil over the whole and, if you have a handful of fresh coriander, chop it finely and place on the top. Mellow in appearance, this dish tastes absolutely delicious.

Sesame Prawns on Toast

Not a traditional recipe from the *hutong*s, but a modern one featuring the seafood that I love. In this starter, the sesame seeds are a perfect complement to the sea-taste and texture of the prawns, the little toasts delicious when served with a glass of cold white or sparkling wine. Sometimes, in my present life, I have to pinch myself: the little boy running down the alley towards the river would not have believed that such luxuries could ever be so readily to hand.

INGREDIENTS

10 big fresh tiger prawns, peeled, deheaded, chopped very, very finely (we say 'mashed') and put in a bowl
1–2 pinches of sea salt
1 teaspoon cooking rice wine
1 egg, beaten
cornflour
sesame seed oil
sesame seeds
white bread, medium-sliced
sunflower oil

METHOD

Put the mashed prawns, salt, cooking rice wine and beaten egg into a bowl and mix well. Add one heaped dessertspoon of cornflour and mix again; then add a few drops of sesame seed oil and mix one more time. Pour a little mountain of sesame seeds on to a plate. Take a slice of white bread (you can use brown if you prefer, but the Chinese always like white) and, using a knife, spread some of the prawn mixture quite thickly and evenly all over one side of the bread, right to the edges. Now place the slice, mixture-side down, on to the sesame seeds, thereby coating the prawn mixture; then set it on another plate, sesame-side up, to await cooking. Repeat this process with further slices until you have finished your mixture.

Heat your wok until it is hot, and add 8 tablespoons of sunflower oil, heating until it is almost smoking. Turning the heat to medium-high, place one slice at a time – bread-only (uncoated) side down first – in the wok and leave for 1–1½ minutes before turning over. The bread-only side should be a golden toasted colour. Now touch this toasted side with your chopsticks; you should hear the crackling *ra-ta-ta-ta-ta* sound of the sesame seeds toasting underneath. After another 1–1½ minutes, lift the toasted slices out of the oil, remove the crusts, cut each slice into 3 equal strips and then each of these in half – making 6 pieces from each slice. If you like you can cut them even smaller, into bite-size delicacies. Have just a few pieces each.

RICE, TO ACCOMPANY YOUR MAIN DISHES

Cooking Your Rice

In China, when we say 'steamed rice', we are actually referring to the traditional method of boiling rice. I have not found a rice as bulky and translucent as my sister Liang's sack of rice since my childhood; now I would suggest that you use fragrant basmati rice to accompany your dishes. The Chinese will put a pan of rice on to the stove almost without thinking, as the prelude to preparing and cooking the main dishes. When I was little, my sisters used to shout, '*Guo Yue! Tao mi zuo-fan!*' ('Guo Yue! Wash the rice and cook it!') They then had time to think about their dishes.

METHOD

Fill 2 English teacups with rice and pour into a medium saucepan. Wash the rice two or three times with water from the tap to remove the starch (traditionally you would wash it between your hands). Now add enough cold water to cover the rice – and then a little more. Level the rice with your hand, then dip your index finger into the water to touch the rice with the tip of your finger. The water should reach the crease marking the joint closest to your fingertip. This is the traditional way of measuring your water for cooking rice. Now place a lid on the pan.

As you begin to prepare and cook your main dishes, put the pan on to a high heat and bring the water to the boil. When the water is boiling (you may need to lift the lid to check, but be sure to replace it immediately), turn the heat down to low and simmer gently while you work on the dishes. The rice is a constant presence. When you can no longer see water in the pan – after about 5–10 minutes – turn the heat down to its absolute lowest, and leave for a further 10–15 minutes. In China, at this point, we put a ring on the stove, to raise the pan of rice above the heat – this is what we mean when we say 'steamed' rice. This creates the distinctive texture.

VEGETABLE DISHES

To me, the beauty and creativity of Chinese home cooking is expressed above all in the simplicity and creativity of the vegetable dishes. I would like all of you one day to visit a market in Beijing, where seasonal vegetables are arranged like jewels, and people spend a long time analysing the purples, reds, oranges, yellows and all shades of white and green, smelling and feeling each vegetable that catches their eye with the senses of a connoisseur. There is a special atmosphere, of freshness, vitality and imagination. Sometimes the vegetables are combined with golden crispy egg, the contrasting tastes and textures working in harmony.

Chao san si

FRIED THREE SILK

A simple, colourful combination of potato, carrot and red and green pepper, quick-fried in oil with rock or sea salt. The key to this dish lies in the very careful preparation and chopping techniques, followed by a fast, controlled performance, creating colours and smells that still evoke that moment in my childhood when I walked into a restaurant for the first time. That day, *chao san si*, which I knew my mother could not afford, was being served on round, flat dishes, painted with many flowers.

INGREDIENTS

2 medium white potatoes, peeled
2 small carrots or 1 medium carrot, peeled
1 small red pepper
1 small green pepper
sunflower oil
2 spring onions, washed and finely chopped
sea salt
Chinese cooking rice wine
sesame seed oil
light soy sauce

METHOD

Begin by slicing the potatoes into very thin rounds; then, piling up a few rounds at a time, slice very finely into thin stick-shapes, the length of matchsticks. Prepare all the potato in this way, then put it into a colander, running cold water over it for some time to wash out the starch; this will prevent your potato from becoming sticky in the cooking process.

Next, prepare the carrot. If you are right-handed, hold the carrot horizontally on the chopping board with your left hand, and cut very thin, diagonal slices, beginning at the far right-hand corner. Then, taking a few slices at a time, cut very finely into sticks, as you did with the potato – the chopping technique we call 'shredding'. Ideally, you should aim for a fast, even rhythm – a very traditional sound in the alleys, but it takes a lot of practice! Pile this carrot on to a plate to await cooking.

Deseed the peppers and slice very finely, once again. The idea is to create more or less identical shapes from the potato, carrot and peppers, although the pepper will naturally be more curved. This is the key to the dish, because it means the cooking process – which we call quick-frying – can be fast and even.

193

Heat your wok until it is hot, add 3 tablespoons of sun-flower oil, and wait until this oil begins to smoke a little; it is now hot enough. Put in all of the finely chopped spring onion, which will make a gentle sound, followed by the carrot and pepper, which will make a good sizzling sound. Then add the potato – which will make an even bigger sound! Move all the ingredients around in the wok and, if possible, toss! Breathe in the aroma: this is the smell of pure vegetables that I remember from my childhood. Add 1 teaspoon of sea salt, and move everything around briskly with a wooden spoon, tossing again. Now taste, to ensure that the vegetables are cooked, but still crunchy; the cooking time should be about 3–4 minutes only, like a fast performance. Finally, add a drizzle of cooking rice wine, sesame seed oil and light soy sauce; the dish is now ready to serve. The colours are beauti-ful: green, orange and pale yellow-gold.

Mu xu cai

WOODLAND DISH

One of my mother's favourites, this woodland dish, in shades of cream, yellow and brown, uses some of the fascinating dried and preserved ingredients in Chinese cooking: bamboo shoots, dried mushrooms, wood-ear and lily-flower, which in my childhood were all highly rationed. By combining them with the *bai-cai* (Chinese leaf), potato and egg, you will create a wonderful harmony of intriguing tastes. The ingredients, like the colours and textures, are beautifully balanced, pro-viding a wealth of nutrition and an earthy intensity, without any extremes. My mother used to say that this dish was a favourite among Buddhist monks, before Buddhism was banned in China.

You need to buy the dried ingredients from a specialist Chinese shop, where they are sold in packets. It is essential to soak them thoroughly, so do this one hour before beginning your other preparation. There are two main kinds of dried wood-ear (tree fungus): one that is big with a thicker texture, another that is small and much finer: try to buy this one. The bamboo shoots required for this recipe are also available from these specialist shops, sliced in water in a tin.

INGREDIENTS

Chinese dried mushrooms, dried wood-ear and dried lily-flower
  (a small handful of each)
2 eggs, well beaten
1 spring onion, washed and very finely chopped
sea salt
sunflower oil
1 small tin of bamboo shoots – remove from the tin, drain and
  chop very finely (the traditional technique we call
  'shredding')
1 large white potato, peeled – cut into very thin slices, then
  shred into very fine matchstick shapes
1 small *bai-cai* (Chinese leaf) – wash and remove the outer
  leaves, then chop very finely
light soy sauce
white caster sugar
Chinese cooking rice wine
1 clove of garlic, peeled, crushed and very finely chopped
sesame seed oil

METHOD

An hour before beginning the rest of your preparation, place the dried ingredients – the Chinese mushrooms, wood-ear and lily-flower – in a bowl, pour hot water from a kettle over them and leave to soak for about an hour. Once they have uncurled and opened, wash them very thoroughly. Then, taking each wood-ear, remove any lumps that you find; these will be 'sandy' inside and are not to be eaten. Then wash them again in a colander and squeeze with your hands to remove the excess water, before slicing your wood-ear if they are large. With the lily-flowers, after soaking them, chop the hard end off each one – this was the flower. Otherwise, keep the natural shapes of these ingredients.

Next, after all your chopping preparation, add half of the spring onion to the beaten eggs in a bowl and then a couple of pinches of salt. Heat your wok, add 2 tablespoons of sunflower oil and continue heating until it begins to smoke. Add the egg mixture and, as it cooks, turning a golden colour, break it up with your chopsticks or spatula. Put to one side. Now pour 3 tablespoons of sunflower oil into the wok and heat until it is just smoking. Add the other half of the spring onion and you should hear a percussive sound; this means your oil is hot enough. Now add all the other prepared vegetables and move around for a few minutes, adding 2 more pinches of salt. Next add the egg and then, stirring continuously, the following in succession: 2 tablespoons of light soy sauce, 1 teaspoon of caster sugar, 2 teaspoons of cooking rice wine, the finely chopped garlic, and a final drizzle of sesame seed oil. The addition of these final five ingredients creates a beautiful depth of taste.

Stir-fried Potato with Sugar, Vinegar and Soy Sauce

A favourite among children, this was the first dish that I learned to cook, under the guidance of my sisters.

INGREDIENTS

2 medium white potatoes, peeled
sunflower oil
1 spring onion, washed and finely chopped
white caster sugar
sea salt
light soy sauce
Chinese dark rice vinegar (I recommend Chinkiang rice vinegar)
sesame seed oil

METHOD

Cut each potato in half across the middle, and then into very fine round slices. Piling up a few of these at a time, cut into very thin matchstick shapes (the technique called 'shredding'). It is essential that the potato is cut this finely, because the cooking time is very short. So this is a good exercise in traditional chopping; try to get an even rhythm. Do not wash the potato at this point, because you want to keep a sticky texture in this dish.

Heat your wok until it is hot, and add 2½ tablespoons of oil. When the oil is very hot, put in the spring onion and, as the percussive sound fades, add the potato, which will make a loud sound over the very high heat. Move the ingredients around in the wok with a wooden spoon, and sprinkle on 3 level teaspoons of sugar, stirring all the time from the bottom to prevent sticking. Add 2 pinches of salt – keep stirring – and then 3 teaspoons of light soy sauce, still stirring.

Drizzle 2 teaspoons of Chinese dark rice vinegar over the potato, stir and taste. This cooking time should be only 2–3 minutes. The potato should be cooked, but still retain a crunchy texture. Finally, add a tiny touch of sesame seed oil, and serve. The success of this dish will depend on your careful preparation.

Chao qie si

FRIED AUBERGINE SILK

This is the simple aubergine dish that my sisters were cooking when I watched them singing and dancing in our home. It uses less oil than other aubergine dishes, and is absolutely delicious when served with steamed rice and maybe some fish. It is a traditional alley dish, and relies on good aubergines, which should have dark glossy purple skins and be firm to the touch.

INGREDIENTS

1 aubergine, peeled unless you have found a very good one,
    with a glossy skin
sunflower oil
1 spring onion, washed and finely chopped
sea salt
light soy sauce
2 cloves of garlic, peeled, crushed and roughly chopped
sesame seed oil

METHOD

First, prepare the aubergine. Cut it in half across the middle and then slice into fine rounds. Piling up a few of these circles at a time, slice finely into stick-shapes, about ½ cm (¼ in) thick and 6 cm (2½ in) long. Now heat your wok until it is hot, add 2 tablespoons of sunflower oil and wait until the oil is just beginning to smoke. Put in the spring onion and then, when the sound has faded, add the aubergine, which will make only a gentle sound. Move it around in the wok, with a wooden spoon if you are using a non-stick wok, a traditional Chinese *chanzi* (metal spatula) if you are using a metal wok. After a minute, turn the heat down a little, otherwise the aubergine will stick to the wok. The aubergine should now be starting to change colour; keep moving it around, adding 2 pinches of salt, followed by 1 dessertspoon of light soy sauce. After 4–5 minutes, put the garlic into the wok, moving the ingredients constantly, and taste. The dish should be lightly flavoured, with a pure vegetable taste. After another minute, add a drizzle of sesame seed oil and taste again. The aubergine should melt in your mouth, with the texture of silk.

Jiu-cai

CHINESE CHIVES WITH EGG

The vivid colour and freshness of summer Chinese chives, like long green, luscious grass, always filled me with delight as a child. You should be able to find them in a specialist Chinese food shop. In this recipe, they are combined with golden, crispy egg to make a fresh, nutritious dish that is typical of Chinese home cooking; you will never find it in a restaurant.

Please note: *jiu-cai* is related to spring onion, which is therefore not necessary in this dish.

INGREDIENTS

a large handful (about 225 g or 8 oz) of *jiu-cai*, known as
    Chinese chives, washed
sunflower oil
2 eggs, beaten with a pinch of salt
sea salt
sesame seed oil

METHOD

First, prepare your *jiu-cai*: holding them as a handful, cut into small pieces, about 2 cm (¾ in) long. Then heat your wok until it is hot, add 3 tablespoons of oil and continue heating until the oil is just beginning to smoke. Put in the beaten eggs and move them briskly around in the wok in all directions for about a minute, until you have golden, crispy pieces. Now add the Chinese chives, together with 3 pinches of sea salt (adjust this to suit your taste), and move them around so as to distribute the heat evenly. They will take only a couple of minutes to cook. Finally, add a drizzle of sesame seed oil; your dish is now ready to serve. It is absolutely delicious with bulky, steamed rice.

Chao tu-dou si

FRIED EARTH-BEAN SILK (POTATO WITH SICHUAN PEPPER)

This is a simple, tasty recipe in which Sichuan peppercorns provide an aromatic edge to what is otherwise a gentle dish, the texture of the potato maintained through careful timing. It is this contrast in strengths that appealed to the *suona* player, like a soft melody interspersed with powerful notes played on another instrument. This is a little dish, to accompany others.

INGREDIENTS

2 medium white potatoes, peeled
sunflower oil
1 spring onion, washed and finely chopped
1 teaspoon Sichuan peppercorns (the reddish brown dried
    berries of the prickly ash tree)
sea salt
Chinese white rice vinegar (Western white wine vinegar also
    works well in this dish)
sesame seed oil

METHOD

First, prepare your potatoes: slice them into thin rounds and then, piling up a few of these at a time, slice very, very finely – the technique we call 'shredding'. You should end up with a pile of very thin matchstick shapes. Put into a colander and run under cold water for a while to remove the starch, so as to prevent the dish from becoming sticky. This preparation is absolutely crucial to the success of your dish.

Heat your wok until it is hot, and then add 3 tablespoons of sunflower oil; continue heating until the oil is very hot, just beginning to smoke. Add the spring onion, which should make a percussive sound, and then the peppercorns; move these around in the wok – they will turn black in a minute or two. Now add your potato – be prepared for a big sound! Move everything briskly around, adding 3-4 pinches of sea salt, and toss if you can! Continue to move it around for a further minute or two, then add a drizzle of light vinegar and the same of sesame seed oil. Toss with a flourish, and taste: the potato should be cooked, but still crunchy. The peppercorns are like black spots of ink in the pale gold potato; in the alleys we eat these, but you might prefer to remove them with your chopsticks. The whole cooking process should be a fast, measured performance.

Egg and Tomato

This simple, delicious dish, which my friend the *suona* player also loved to cook, has a surprisingly rich taste. It is a great favourite in Chinese home cooking, especially in the Beijing alleys, and can be accompanied by steamed rice or *man-tou*. It's one of the quickest dishes to prepare, and children always love it.

INGREDIENTS

10 ripe tomatoes
4 eggs
2 spring onions, washed and finely chopped
sunflower oil
white caster sugar
light soy sauce
sea salt
sesame seed oil

METHOD

Try to choose ripe tomatoes – red, and not hard. Wash them and cut each into about 6 to 8 segments, like narrow little boats. Place to one side. Next, break the eggs into a bowl and beat thoroughly. Add the finely chopped spring onion and mix. Heat your wok and add 3 tablespoons of sunflower oil, turning the heat to high. Wait until the oil is just beginning to smoke – the timing is important – and then add the egg mixture. You should hear a good sound, as the egg immediately begins to rise and then to crisp; without this sound, without the correct heat, the egg will be flat and rubbery. Using a spatula, turn and break up the egg. In my childhood, we used the metal spatula known as a *chanzi* for this; the sound it made against the inside of the wok was traditionally a familiar one in the courtyards, distracting children from their games with the promise of good food. Nowadays, with non-stick woks and wooden spoons, we have lost this special sound. Once you have turned the egg, let it fry for another minute or two, stirring all the time.

With the heat still high, pour the tomato on to the egg in the wok and stir for a further half a minute. Add 1½ dessert-spoons of sugar and mix; then add 1 dessertspoon of light soy sauce and a pinch of sea salt, mixing once more. Turn the heat down a little and allow to cook for 2–3 minutes, until the tomato is soft and has absorbed all the flavours. Drizzle a few drops of sesame seed oil on to the egg and tomato, and put into a serving bowl. The sauce, comprising the juices of the tomato and all the flavouring ingredients, is especially delicious with the rice or *man-tou*.

Three Colours: Aubergine with Tomatoes and Mange-tout

A beautiful example of colour and texture in Chinese home cooking. In this simple dish, the red of the tomato contrasts with the deep green of the mange-tout and the silky earth-tones of the aubergine. Each individual taste and texture stands out, but they also blend perfectly together. In the summer, I used to like growing mange-tout in my courtyard, alongside green beans – more bulky than any I can find now – and *si gua* (silk melon), which looks like a cucumber and is similar to a courgette; inside it is like cotton.

Try to find a very dark purple aubergine, ideally without too many seeds inside, as their presence often means it will be difficult to cook, being overripe and not tender. In Chinese markets aubergines come in many different shapes and depths of colour. People spend a long time selecting the right one. If you choose well, the aubergine in this dish will melt in your mouth.

INGREDIENTS

1 dark purple aubergine, washed but not peeled
3 tomatoes, washed and unpeeled
sunflower oil
1 × 150 g (5½ oz) packet of mange-tout, trimmed by hand
light soy sauce
white caster sugar
1 clove of garlic, peeled, crushed and finely chopped
1 spring onion, washed and roughly chopped
sea salt
sesame seed oil

METHOD

Begin by preparing the aubergine. First remove the rough end of the vegetable; then cut the aubergine in half lengthwise, and each segment in half again and then again, until you have 8 segments. Taking one segment at a time, cut a medium-thin diagonal slice at one end; then roll the aubergine away from yourself, as if taking one step, following the chiselled shape of the aubergine, and make another diagonal slice, about 2½ cm (1 in) thick, beside the first. Continue to turn the aubergine over and slice in this way, until you have finished one segment. You should have a collection of multi-faceted shapes, which the Chinese say are like diamonds (measuring 5 cm or 2 in in length). This is the traditional *gun-dao* (rolling vegetable knife) technique. Prepare all the aubergine in this way.

Next, prepare the tomatoes. Cut each one in half, down the centre, and then in half again, and then one more time, so that again you have 8 segments from each. With the spring onion and mange-tout, you are now ready to cook.

Heat your wok until it is hot and add 3 tablespoons of sunflower oil. When the oil is hot, but not smoking (this is important when you are cooking aubergine, because of its special texture), add the aubergine diamonds. Stir for a couple of minutes, to coat all the aubergine with oil. Remember that aubergine absorbs a lot of oil, so if it seems to be getting too dry, add a further drizzle, but not too much; then turn the heat down to below medium. You have to be patient with aubergine! Turn and stir the diamond shapes constantly until they become soft; this should take about 5–8 minutes. Then turn the heat down to low. Continue cooking for 2–3 minutes, stirring occasionally.

Now turn the heat back up to medium and add the mange-tout and tomatoes. Stir from time to time, for about 3 minutes. Then add 1 tablespoon of light soy sauce and 1 teaspoon of sugar, followed by the garlic, spring onion and a few pinches of salt. Keep stirring for another couple of minutes, or until the aubergine is soft but still textured. Finally add a drizzle of sesame seed oil. The dish is now ready; serve it with steamed rice.

Suan-rong bo-cai

RED-STEMMED SPINACH WITH CRUSHED GARLIC

The notion of natural simplicity in cooking a philosophy that I learned and shared with my friend the *suona* player. You must buy the fresh spinach, still with its red-tipped green stems, as it is when it comes out of the earth, not only the leaves. In China we eat the green stalks. This dish is beautiful for your body.

INGREDIENTS

sunflower oil
2–3 cloves of garlic, peeled, crushed and very finely chopped
1 packet of spinach, about 250 g (9 oz), washed thoroughly, the
     red tips removed, the rest torn roughly into pieces
sea salt
sesame seed oil

METHOD

Heat the wok until it is hot, and add 2 tablespoons of sunflower oil. Wait until your oil is just beginning to smoke and then add the chopped garlic. Next put in the spinach, and ideally toss it – or move it around inside the wok – so that it heats evenly. Add 2 pinches of sea salt and a drizzle of sesame seed oil. The process is a fast, controlled performance! The spinach leaves should be a deep forest-green colour, the stalks a lighter green. The intensity of the colour depends on the timing.

MEAT AND POULTRY

Pork was the main source of meat in my childhood: a luxury that was highly rationed. Many of the traditional alley dishes reflect this: the pork is used with great imagination and ingenuity, often in disguise – as an unexpected, delicious taste – or combined with seasonal vegetables to create contrasting notes of intense flavour. The most famous dish in the alleys, though, was my mother's favourite, red stewed pork. I am also including in this section two chicken recipes that my sisters love, using the traditional tastes of peanut, sesame seed paste and chilli; and one beef recipe, which evokes the friendships of my later childhood.

Hong shao rou

RED STEWED PORK WITH *FEN-TIAO* OR *FEN-SI* (DRIED BEAN NOODLES)

Much loved by my mother, from her childhood in Harbin, *hong shao rou* is a dark, aromatic dish, perfect when served with steaming rice and wine. The smell is so distinctive, it would travel through the courtyards and narrow alleys like music, evoking them to this day.

Fen-tiao are the traditional accompaniment to *hong shao rou*. Originally shaped like flat ribbons but nowadays more rounded, like dried noodles, they are made from beans or sweet potato. If you cannot find these in a specialist shop, you can use *fen-si* (glass noodles or green-bean threads, made from mung beans) instead; these, however, will take less time to cook, as I mention below. In this recipe, you can use dried flour noodles or fresh, hand-made noodles.

INGREDIENTS

280 g (10 oz) belly of pork – this provides just the right combination of lean and fat, but do use leaner pork if you prefer (you can also increase the amount of pork, if you like, but remember that you will have other lighter dishes on the table, such as green beans and *bai-cai*)
sunflower oil
white caster sugar
30 g (1 oz) piece of ginger, unpeeled and sliced into 4 pieces
dark soy sauce (or light soy sauce, if you prefer – the dark variety is stronger and more traditional)
cooking rice wine
4 pieces of cinnamon bark
4 star anise
2 big, or 4 small, spring onions, roughly chopped
hot water from the kettle
sea salt
2 handfuls (about 150 g or 5½ oz) of *fen-tiao* or *fen-si* (dried bean noodles)

METHOD

Begin by cutting the pork into slices, about 4 cm (1½ in) long, 2 cm (¾ in) thick. Then heat your wok until it is hot, and add 2 tablespoons of sunflower oil over a medium-high heat. When the oil is hot, add 2 dessertspoons of sugar, stirring so that the sugar really melts and turns a slightly reddish colour. Add the pork and move the pieces around so that they become coated with the sugar glaze. After a couple of minutes, the pork will have changed colour as the oil has bubbled around it. Keep moving the meat around for another couple of minutes, before transferring to a medium-size saucepan; don't add any more oil. Now put in the four slices of ginger, 3 tablespoons of soy sauce and ½ dessert-spoon of cooking rice wine; these ingredients should be simmering in the pan. Add the cinnamon bark, star anise, spring onion and 3 tablespoons of hot water from the kettle, and mix, before turning the heat down to medium-low. Sprinkle on 1 teaspoon of sea salt. Place a lid on the pan, and leave to simmer.

Now prepare the *fen-tiao* or *fen-si*. Pour some just-boiled water into another saucepan, and put in the dried noodles, keeping them submerged as they absorb the water and begin to soften. Move them around with your chopsticks to make sure they are completely covered by the water, and leave. We call this process *tang-tang* (soak in).

The pork and other ingredients should now have been simmering for 7–8 minutes. Removing the lid for a moment, add 3 tablespoons of hot water and leave to simmer again. After a further 5 minutes, add another 3 tablespoons of hot water, stir and then leave once again. Repeat this procedure after another 5 minutes, to prevent the ingredients from becoming dry, but to retain their intensity of flavour.

The noodles should now be silky in texture; transfer them to a colander to drain. In my childhood, the meat had to stew for 1½–2 hours before it was tender – and utterly delicious. The pigs had roamed so freely in the countryside, wandering around the villages, eating whatever they came across; the resulting meat was somehow stronger, tastier. Nowadays, the pork becomes tender much more quickly, but to my mind it has lost something of that pure, free taste.

After a further 5 minutes, add another 3 tablespoons of hot water; then, after 5 more minutes, put the *fen-tiao* or *fen-si* into the pan, at this point adding 10 tablespoons of hot water. After 3–4 minutes, if you are using *fen-si* (the lighter glass noodles) your dish will be ready. If you are using *fen-tiao*, however, you will need now to add a further 5 tablespoons of hot water and then simmer for another 2–3 minutes.

Make sure you taste this dish before serving it; the noodles, which will be a rich burnt-sienna colour, just like the pork (lighter in colour if you are using light soy sauce), should be full of all the flavours you have added – the star anise, cinnamon, rice wine and ginger. The cooking time, from the moment you begin simmering the pork with all these flavouring ingredients, should be about 35 minutes if you are using *fen-tiao*, a little shorter if you are using *fen-si*. Serve with steamed rice.

Qie he

AUBERGINE BOX

This is a famous Beijing dish: aubergine boxes (similar in shape to traditional Chinese purses) with the hidden taste of pork, seasoned with beautiful flavours. Being unexpected, the taste is more intense. When you choose your aubergines, try to find very dark purple ones; the Chinese like to judge a vegetable by its colour. In my childhood, we didn't need to peel our aubergines because the skins were so delicious; they had just arrived on carts from the countryside, all shapes and sizes – some completely round! Now I find I have to peel most aubergines.

INGREDIENTS

For the boxes

2 medium aubergines, peeled unless you have found very
  beautiful ones

For the stuffing

300 g (11 oz) free-range or organic minced pork (you can
  include 10 tiger prawns, peeled and very finely chopped, if
  you wish, with a little less pork, say 225 g or 8 oz)
2 spring onions, washed, cut into very thin strips, and then very
  finely chopped
2½ teaspoons very finely chopped ginger (about 7–8 very thin
  slices from a medium bulb)
1 teaspoon Chinese cooking rice wine
3 pinches of sea salt
1 dessertspoon light soy sauce
1 dessertspoon cornflour
1 egg white

For cooking the stuffed boxes

sunflower oil

For the seasoning

light soy sauce
Chinese cooking rice wine
white caster sugar
warm water from the kettle
1 spring onion, washed and finely chopped
1 clove of garlic, peeled and finely chopped

METHOD

First, make the stuffing. Mix the pork, 2 of the chopped spring
onions and the chopped ginger together very thoroughly in a

bowl. Now add the following ingredients, one by one: 1 teaspoon of Chinese cooking rice wine, 3 pinches of sea salt, 1 dessertspoon of light soy sauce and 1 dessertspoon of cornflour (to keep the pork tender). Next, add the egg white and mix again thoroughly. Have the remainder of the ingredients to hand.

Next, prepare the aubergines. Peel them and cut them in half across the middle – the equator, as it were. Taking one half and resting it on your chopping board, begin to cut a thin slice - circular, of course, and about ½ cm (¼ in) thick – but stop three-quarters of the way down, so that the slice is still attached to rest of the aubergine. Then cut another thin slice immediately next to the first one, which is still attached; but this time cut the new slice off completely. The two circular slices will be joined together, allowing you to put some stuffing inside. This is your aubergine box. Continue to prepare the remainder of the aubergine in this way until you have a collection of these boxes.

Put one heaped teaspoon of the stuffing into each box, flattening the mixture evenly like butter. Of course, some boxes will be bigger than others. Close each box, and put them all on a plate, ready for cooking.

Turning the heat up to high, heat the wok until it is hot. Then add 2 tablespoons of oil, moving the wok to spread the oil around, and turn the heat down to medium-high. When the oil is hot, place the aubergine boxes flat on the bottom of the wok, as many as will form one layer of boxes; they should make a sizzling sound. After 1–2 minutes, the boxes should have a brown, toasted appearance on one side; now remove them from the wok. Add 2 more tablespoons of oil and, when it is hot, return the boxes to the wok to cook the other sides. Turning the heat down a little more, cook for another 2–3 minutes until the boxes are brown and soft. Cook all the aubergine boxes in this way, one layer at a time. Then turn your heat down to low, and put all the cooked aubergine back into the wok.

You are now ready to add the seasoning: 1 tablespoon of light soy sauce, 1 teaspoon of cooking rice wine, 1½ dessert-spoons of sugar and 2 tablespoons of warm water from the kettle. Allow the ingredients to simmer on a medium-low heat for 5 minutes. Then put in the remaining finely chopped spring onion and the garlic, and continue to simmer. Add one more tablespoon of water and cover the wok with a lid, allowing the dish to simmer for 2 more minutes. Serve with steamed rice, alongside some fresh, seasonal vegetables such as green beans.

Jiang-dou

FOUR-SEASON OR SNAKE BEANS WITH PORK AND CRUSHED GARLIC

You should be able to find these special long green, often coiled, beans in a Chinese food shop. Combined with crushed garlic and tiny pieces of pork, which add delightful notes of contrast to the emerald-green freshness of the beans, they make a truly delicious dish. I loved to make this in my brick kitchen, tasting it many times before presenting it to the family! You can, if you like, use other green beans in this recipe, though the taste won't be quite as irresistible. I also like to cook *suan-tai* (garlic shoots or stems) in this way – another fresh, distinctive, seasonal dish.

INGREDIENTS

sunflower oil
1 spring onion, very finely chopped (remember to use both green and white parts)
85 g (3 oz) minced pork
10–12 *jiang-dou* beans, cut into pieces 2 cm (¾ in) long – hold the

beans together with one hand and cut them with your other
hand (always a good feeling, I think)

sea salt

1 large clove of garlic, or 2 smaller cloves, peeled, crushed and
very finely chopped (I love the traditional sound of chopping;
the wooden chopping board itself moves in a fast, even
rhythm against the surface of a wooden table when the
technique is correct.)

light soy sauce

METHOD

Heat your wok until it is hot, add two tablespoons of sunflower oil and continue to heat until it is medium-hot. Add
the spring onion – which should make a percussive sound –
and then the pork, stirring your ingredients all the time and
pressing the meat down into the wok for a minute, to separate
the little pieces of pork. Then transfer the contents of the wok
to a small bowl. Into the wok pour a little more sunflower oil
– around half a tablespoon – and, once the oil is medium-hot,
put in the beans, together with two pinches of sea salt, shov-
elling all the time with a wooden spatula. After 5 minutes add
the garlic, along with your pork and spring onion, moving all
the ingredients around for 1-2 minutes. Finally, add a drizzle
of light soy sauce.

Diced Pork with Potato and Carrot

I have always liked the element of disguise in this dish: the
three main ingredients are all cut into similar shapes and
sizes and then coated in dark soy sauce, with a sprinkling
of sugar. As you hold a piece between your chopsticks, you
are unsure as to whether it is pork, carrot or potato, and
this uncertainty seems to intensify the taste. The carrot in

particular has a beautiful sweetness. The key to this dish lies in the chopping techniques.

INGREDIENTS

1 large potato, peeled
2 medium carrots, peeled
sunflower oil
cornflour
1 spring onion, washed and finely chopped
110 g (4 oz) free-range or organic diced pork, cut into little cubes
dark soy sauce
white caster sugar (you can use brown if you prefer, but the Chinese use only white)
sea salt
2 cloves of garlic, peeled, crushed and finely chopped

METHOD

Begin by preparing the potato. Cut it lengthwise into 4 segments – more if it is very round. Then cut each segment into small angled shapes, using the *gun-dao* (rolling vegetable knife) technique: each time you cut, roll the potato away from you and cut, alternating the angle of the knife each time so that you create small pieces of potato that have different-shaped sides (diamonds, squares) – almost as if you were cutting a precious stone! Prepare the carrot in a similar way: cut in half across the middle, and then cut into small angled shapes, about 2 cm (¾ in) long, using the same traditional technique.

Heat your wok until it is hot, add 3 tablespoons of sunflower oil and wait until the oil is beginning to smoke. Put the carrot in first – being the hardest it takes longest to cook – and move it around in the wok. After 2 minutes, add the potato, and reduce the heat to medium-high. Cook for about 12 minutes, until the potato has become golden. Now put these vegetables into a dish.

Mix 2 teaspoons of cornflour with 2 drops of cold water, to coat the little cubes of pork. Now add half of the finely chopped spring onion to the hot oil remaining in the wok; when the sound has faded – after about a minute – put the pork into the wok, stirring it briskly to move it around as it changes to a pale colour. After a couple of minutes, return the potato and carrot to the wok. Add ½ tablespoon of dark soy sauce, followed by 3 teaspoons of sugar, evenly sprinkled over the ingredients. Keep stirring all the time to heat everything uniformly, and add a pinch of salt. Finally put in the finely chopped garlic, and cook for a further 1–2 minutes. Transfer to a dish, and serve with steamed rice.

Hong shao dou-fu

RED STEWED BEAN CURD WITH PORK

I remember eating this traditional dish with friends in the restaurants of Bei-hai Park and the Summer Palace. The *dou-fu* changes in the cooking process, first from white to gold and then to a reddish golden-brown colour. Like a blank canvas to which pigments are gradually added, the bean curd acquires all the beautiful flavours of the other ingredients. Delicious with steamed rice.

INGREDIENTS

sea salt
150 g (5½ oz) organic or free-range pork, cut into fine strips
half of 1 egg white
cornflour

ingredients continue ➤

sunflower oil
1 pack of fresh *dou-fu* (bean curd), cut into slices, 1½ cm (½–¾ in)
    thick
1 spring onion, finely chopped
20 mange-tout
a large handful of small, frozen peas
1 carrot, finely chopped
½ red pepper and ½ green pepper, thinly sliced or preferably torn
    by hand into little pieces
light soy sauce
warm water from the kettle
white caster sugar
2 cloves of garlic, crushed and finely chopped
Chinese cooking rice wine
sesame seed oil
fresh coriander, finely chopped

METHOD

First, add a very little sea salt to the pork strips in a bowl,
together with half an egg white and two teaspoons of cornflour, and mix well together, coating the meat. Leave to one
side while you fry the *dou-fu*.

Heat your wok until it is hot, add 4 tablespoons of sunflower oil and wait until the oil is just beginning to smoke.
Using chopsticks, put in your *dou-fu* slices one by one; they
should make a beautiful percussive sound as they dance in the
hot oil. Lift your wok above the stove and move it around, tilting it gently, to coat the bean curd evenly. Then return it to the
high heat. The oil should be bubbling around the *dou-fu*,
which we describe as being 'cold' because it can take so much
heat; underneath it should be turning golden. *Dou-fu* is very
special: it is cooked by the hot oil, but its texture means that
it doesn't absorb the oil, only the colours, tastes and smells of
the ingredients that you add to it. This first side will take

about 6 minutes to toast properly. Only then should you turn the *dou-fu* over to cook the other side; after about 4 more minutes the bean curd will be a beautiful golden-brown colour. When the surface of both sides is crispy, remove the *dou-fu* from the wok and keep to one side, leaving the remaining oil.

Add a little more sunflower oil, wait until it is hot, and then add the spring onion – which should make a good percussive sound – followed by the pork, moving the meat around briskly as it rapidly changes colour. After about a minute, add the mange-tout, peas, carrot and red and green pepper, all prepared carefully in advance; these will add taste and colour to the dish. Keep moving the ingredients around, as you add 2 pinches of sea salt. Now return the crispy *dou-fu* to the wok and keep stirring. Drizzle 1½ dessertspoons of light soy sauce over the ingredients, followed by 3 tablespoons of warm water from the kettle and 1 teaspoon of sugar, stirring all the time as the dish simmers in the wok for a couple of minutes. Then add the finely chopped garlic and 1½ teaspoons of rice wine. Toss the contents of the wok if you can, to combine all the aromas and flavours. Finally, add a drizzle of sesame seed oil and a little of the fresh, finely chopped coriander. Serve with steamed rice. A very traditional dish in the alleys.

Qing zheng wan-zi

PURE STEAMED PEARL BALLS (STEAMED PORK AND PRAWN BALLS)

This is a very pure, steamed dish from the Qing Dynasty, a beautiful combination of pork and prawns on a simple bed of Chinese leaf. We call it *qing zheng wan-zi*, meaning 'pure steamed pearl balls', because of their pale, delicate, shiny appearance when cooked. I used to make this dish alongside

217

my friend the *suona* player in our courtyard; lightness and tenderness are the qualities you should aim for. Perfect with steamed rice.

INGREDIENTS

12 tiger prawns, peeled and deheaded
175 g (6¼ oz) organic or free-range pork
1 spring onion, finely chopped
4 slices of ginger, very finely chopped
1 heaped dessertspoon cornflour
1 teaspoon Chinese cooking rice wine
½ teaspoon sea salt
1 dessertspoon cold water
1 egg white, whisked
1 *bai-cai* (Chinese leaf), the inside leaves

METHOD

Holding a heavy knife at both ends (using both hands), chop and mash the prawns and pork, going up and down with a fast, regular rhythm until the meat has a fine, even texture. Add the finely chopped spring onion to the mixture, followed by the chopped ginger. Then mix in the cornflour and cooking rice wine, followed by the salt, cold water and egg white. Mix together. Line the base of your bamboo steamer – I use the smaller-size steamer – with the upper half of five leaves taken from the inside of the *bai-cai* and then, using a teaspoon, form little balls from the pork and prawn mixture, each about the size of a cherry tomato. Arrange about 7 of these on the leaves. Put another 2 or 3 leaves on top to form another layer, and on this arrange the same number of balls as before. Add one more layer of *bai-cai*, and on top of this a final arrangement of pork and prawn balls, before placing the lid firmly on your steamer. Put the steamer on to a saucepan of water on the stove and, once the water is boiling, steam for about 10 minutes on a medium-high heat, until the balls appear tight, with a whitish sheen. To serve, put a flat plate underneath the steamer and bring to the table.

Chicken with Red Pepper, Cucumber, Peanuts and Chilli

This is a traditional dish in the *hutong*s, and one that my sisters liked to cook on the few occasions when they were able to obtain chicken. It is fresh and colourful, with the special combination of peanuts and chilli, two of the foundation tastes in my childhood. The traditional recipe features red and green pepper, but I like to use red pepper with cucumber, which gives a fresh, more unusual taste. Feel free to choose whichever tempts you more.

INGREDIENTS

a handful or 2 big tablespoons of raw shelled peanuts
sunflower oil
sea salt
1 large chicken breast, preferably free-range or organic, about 150 g (5½ oz)
1 egg white
cornflour
ground black pepper
Chinese cooking rice wine
1 spring onion, washed and finely chopped
1 teaspoon very finely chopped fresh ginger
1 fresh, long red chilli and 1 long green chilli (adjust or omit according to taste), finely chopped

ingredients continue ➤

½ medium red pepper, washed, deseeded and torn roughly by
   hand into small pieces about 1½–2 cm (¾ in) long
¼ cucumber, washed but not peeled, and cut into cubes, similar
   in size to the red pepper, *or* ½ medium green pepper,
   prepared in the same way as the red pepper
white caster sugar
light soy sauce
sesame seed oil

METHOD

First, cook the peanuts. Heat your wok on a medium-high
heat until it is hot, add 2 tablespoons of oil, and wait until the
oil is hot. Then put the peanuts into the wok and stir, turning
the heat down to medium-low. Move the nuts around, so that
they are all coated, and then stir slowly from side to side; you
should hear a little crackling sound. They will be ready in
about 3 minutes. Drain them in a metal sieve, then put them
into a bowl. Sprinkle a little sea salt over the peanuts and leave
them while you prepare the chicken.

Cut the chicken breast into long strips and then into little
cubes. Put these into a bowl and break the egg white over the
top. Add 2 level teaspoons of cornflour and mix with your
fingers, to coat all the chicken, adding a pinch of sea salt and
a little black pepper, followed by 1 teaspoon of cooking rice
wine; then mix again. Reheat your wok – which is still coated
with oil from the peanuts – and add 2 further tablespoons of
oil over a high heat. When the oil is very hot, put in the
chicken cubes, moving them around constantly; in about one
minute they will change in colour to white. Remove the
chicken from the wok and place in a colander.

Heat the remaining oil in the wok until it is just beginning
to smoke. Now add the finely chopped spring onion, ginger
and chilli, waiting for the sound to fade and the chilli to
change colour. After about 30 seconds, put in the red pepper

and cucumber (or the red and green pepper), followed by 2 pinches of salt. Now return the chicken to your wok, adding a pinch of sugar. Move the ingredients briskly around in the wok, and add the cooked peanuts, tossing two or three times. Finally, add 1 tablespoon of light soy sauce, followed by a drizzle of cooking rice wine and another of sesame seed oil. Toss again, and serve with steamed rice. The pale colour and tenderness of the chicken contrast with the brightness and textures of the pepper and cucumber, the glossy peanuts adding a further note to both taste and texture.

Zhi ma jiang ji

SESAME SEED PASTE CHICKEN

Sometimes my sisters would send me out to buy sesame seed paste. Carrying a little porcelain bowl, I would walk down the alley to the grocery shop: '*Er liang zhi ma jiang*' ('Two *liang* [about two ounces] of sesame seed paste'), I would say in a loud voice, to defeat my shyness. The paste, made from sesame seeds, sugar and peanut oil, was kept in a big pot. I loved to watch the man lifting his ladle, full of the dark-ochre-coloured paste, out of the pot and bounce it lightly in the air for a minute, to let the drops of thick, fragrant liquid, like fluid clay, fall back into the pot. You could breathe in the smell ... it is one of the most evocative aromas from my childhood.

Sesame seed paste, which you can find in specialist Chinese food shops (sold as 'sesame sauce' in a glass jar), is very important in traditional home cooking. Used a lot with flour noodles or glass noodles (made from mung beans), especially in the summer when it is combined with cucumber, the paste is also put inside pancakes and steamed buns, shaped like flowers, and used to flavour meat dishes – in

221

this recipe, chicken with spring onion. This is a very simple, healthy dish, delicious when cold. My children love it without the chilli, so consider this as an alternative option. In this recipe, I will show you how to make your own natural chilli oil; my sisters Kai and Xuan, who grew up in the Sichuan province, would also add Sichuan pepper oil, made in the same way, to this dish.

The heat of the chicken is perfectly complemented by a simple dish of fried *dou-fu* (bean curd), cut into strips and served cold with finely chopped spring onion and a drizzle of very good soy sauce. This is very refreshing.

INGREDIENTS

2 skinless chicken breasts, preferably free-range or organic, together weighing about 280 g (10 oz)
sesame seed paste (or sesame sauce) – you can buy this from a specialist shop
white caster sugar
4 spring onions, washed – cut them in half across the middle and use only the white/pale green parts
light soy sauce
sesame seed oil
cold water
sunflower oil
1 fresh red chilli and 1 fresh green chilli (adjust or omit according to taste), sliced very finely into circles

METHOD

First, bring a medium-size pan of water to the boil; when the water is boiling, put in the chicken breasts, which will take about 10–12 minutes to cook, becoming beautifully white.

Meanwhile, make your sauce: put 1½ teaspoons of sesame seed paste into a porcelain bowl, bouncing the spoon lightly to let the drops return to the pot (remember to smell it – delicious!). Add 1 teaspoon of sugar and mix well.

Remove the chicken from the pan and, placing it on a wooden board, bang it gently with a wooden rolling pin; this will loosen the meat, allowing you to separate it with your fingers into small strips, about 5 cm (2 in) long. Arrange these strips on a nice big plate.

Then, taking the white/pale green parts of the spring onion, slice them lengthwise into very fine strips, to complement the shape of the chicken, and arrange them on top of the meat.

Now, returning to your sauce, add 2 teaspoons of light soy sauce and a drizzle of sesame seed oil, mixing well before adding 2 teaspoons of cold water, mixing again to a brown colour.

Next, make your own chilli oil. Put 1 tablespoon of sunflower oil into a hot wok and heat until it is just beginning to smoke. Add the chilli circles – they should make a big sound – and stir for about a minute. Remove from the heat and allow to cool for a moment before adding the oil (and the chilli, if you like) to your sauce. Mix well and pour evenly over the chicken and spring onion. The dish is now ready to serve; it can be eaten hot or cold, with steamed rice. Perfect for a summer's evening.

Shuang jiao niu rou

BEEF WITH RED AND GREEN PEPPER

I remember eating this dish in the home of my friend Ai Tie Wen, who lived with his father, brother and sister in the alleys; his mother had died when he was very small. I loved to go to his home, to look through his father's books and paintings, to talk about what we wanted to do with our lives, to eat dishes that my family could not afford because there were so many of us. Beef was expensive and highly rationed, the taste truly organic – enriched in this dish by the bright colours and texture of the red and green pepper.

INGREDIENTS

170 g (6 oz) fillet of beef, preferably organic – cut into very fine slices and then, piling up a few of these at a time, cut again into very fine strips (the traditional method known as 'shredding')
Chinese cooking rice wine (I recommend Shaoxing rice wine)
light soy sauce
cornflour
cold water
1 red and 1 green pepper, small to medium in size, washed and then – one quarter at a time – chopped into very thin strips, about 7–8 cm (3 in) long, to complement the beef in shape
2 cloves of garlic, peeled and very finely chopped
2 spring onions, washed and finely chopped
sunflower oil
sea salt
white caster sugar

METHOD

First, marinade the beef: put the shredded meat in a bowl, add 2 teaspoons of Chinese cooking rice wine, 1 teaspoon or a drizzle of light soy sauce, 2 teaspoons of cornflour and 1 dessertspoon of cold water. Work these ingredients into the meat with your fingers, as though giving a massage. Now leave for 20 minutes.

Meanwhile, prepare the peppers, garlic and spring onions. When the beef is ready to be cooked, heat your wok and add

2½ tablespoons of sunflower oil. When the oil is hot, add the meat, moving it briskly around in the wok and using your chopsticks, *chanzi* or spatula to separate the pieces of beef, which will take about 2 minutes to change colour and develop their individual tastes. Then add the garlic and spring onion, followed by the red and green pepper, and move all the ingredients around for a further 1–2 minutes. Now drizzle on 2 teaspoons of light soy sauce and toss, followed by 2 pinches of sea salt and 1 pinch of sugar. Taste. Toss or shovel the ingredients for a further 2 minutes, before serving with steamed rice. Delicious!

FISH AND SEAFOOD

There is a lightness and simplicity about fish and seafood that I have always loved. The tastes and textures combine beautifully with fresh seasonal vegetables, together with the special dried ingredients and unique flavouring notes of Chinese home cooking. Controlling the range and depth of tastes is to me like writing music.

Hong shao yu

RED STEWED FISH

This is the favourite traditional method for cooking yellow flower fish in my family. It is also a good recipe for sea bass, sea bream, organic trout or grey mullet. The dish has an exceptionally strong, deep taste, a rich aroma and a very dark reddish colour. It is delicious when served alongside lighter, green vegetable dishes, or *dou-fu*; its depth is then perfectly counterbalanced.

INGREDIENTS

sunflower oil
1 whole fish, about 400–450 g (14 oz–1 lb), cleaned inside and
    out, with fins and scales removed – score the fish on both sides
ginger, washed but not peeled, 12–15 little slices
3 cloves of garlic, crushed but not chopped
1 spring onion, washed and cut into thin strips (both white and
    green parts)
Chinese dark vinegar (I use Chinkiang rice vinegar)
Chinese cooking wine (I use Shaoxing cooking rice wine)
dark soy sauce
water
white caster sugar
star anise (or alternatively Chinese Five Spice)
sesame seed oil
a little fresh coriander, finely chopped

METHOD

Begin by heating a dry wok, before adding 4 tablespoons of
sunflower oil and heating until very hot. When you put your
fish into the oil, there should be a really dramatic sound! Let
it sit in the oil as you turn the wok around in the air, tilting it
gently to coat the fish evenly; we call this 'giving the fish a hot
bath'. After a minute, turn the fish over; the cooked side
should look nicely toasted. Turn the heat down to medium-
low and cook for 6 minutes.

Meanwhile, put the prepared ginger, garlic and spring
onion into a bowl, and add 2 tablespoons of dark vinegar,
½ tablespoon of cooking wine, 1½ tablespoons of dark soy sauce
and 3 tablespoons of water; mix all these ingredients together.
Then sprinkle on ¼ tablespoon of sugar, and add 2 star anise
– or alternatively 2 pinches of Chinese Five Spice (dried cinnamon, fennel, star anise, ginger and cloves), which also gives
a good flavour. Now pour the sauce onto the fish and cover

with a lid, leaving to to simmer gently on a medium-low heat for 10 minutes. Lastly, drizzle a little sesame seed oil over the fish, and serve with some finely chopped coriander on the top, to add a final touch of fresh, vibrant colour that contrasts well with the astonishingly dark, richly flavoured sauce.

Jiao zhi yu

POUR SAUCE FISH (FISH WITH VEGETABLE SAUCE)

A lighter traditional recipe for *huang hua yu*, our yellow flower fish from the sea. This recipe also works well for organic trout, sea bass, grey mullet or sea bream. The key to this dish lies in the careful preparation of vegetables and dried ingredients, to make a sauce which as a child I used to think was like a padded cotton bedcover, with many different colours sewn together.

You will find the dried lily-flower and wood-ear in a specialist Chinese shop, sold in packets. Be sure to soak and wash them thoroughly in advance, as described below.

INGREDIENTS

½ carrot, peeled
1 strip of red pepper
1 strip of green pepper
a few dried lily-flowers, soaked in hot water from the kettle for about an hour
a few dried wood-ear (tree fungus), soaked with the lily-flower, as above
2 spring onions, washed and finely chopped

ingredients continue ➤

2 chillies; 1 red, 1 green, finely chopped (optional)
1 small piece of ginger (about 10 g or ⅓ oz), peeled and finely
    chopped
2 cloves of garlic, peeled and finely chopped
1 medium fish, about 400–450 g (14 oz–1 lb), cleaned inside and
    out, with the scales and fins removed, scored on both sides
plain flour, to coat the fish
sunflower oil
sea salt
white caster sugar
light soy sauce
hot water from the kettle
Chinese white rice vinegar (or you can use Western white wine
    vinegar)
Chinese cooking rice wine
cornflour
sesame seed oil

METHOD

First, prepare your vegetables. Cut the carrot into very fine
slices, then pile up a few slices at a time and 'shred' them into
long matchstick shapes. Holding these in a neat line, cut into
tiny squares resembling cross-hatching or weaving. Cut the
strips of red and green pepper in the same way, so that you
have equal piles of these tiny squares, in orange, red and green.

When the dried ingredients have soaked properly, wash
them thoroughly using a colander and warm water, removing
any lumps you may find in the wood-ear. Now chop both the
lily-flowers and the wood-ear very finely, and add this handful
to your plate of vegetables, together with the finely chopped
spring onion, ginger and garlic.

Your wok needs to be very clean for this dish. First, before
you start cooking, coat your fish in some plain flour on a
plate. Heat the wok until it is hot, add 4 tablespoons of

sunflower oil, and wait until the oil is really smoking before placing your fish in it. Move the wok in the air to ensure that one side of the fish is properly coated with the hot oil – move first to the tail of the fish, then towards the head. After a minute of cooking on the high heat, turn the fish over to cook for another minute on the other side. Then turn it again, moving the wok once more. After a couple of minutes, turn and cook for a further two minutes. When the fish has turned a beautiful golden-brown colour, remove it from the wok and place on a serving dish. Cooking the fish in this way should take a total of 6–8 minutes.

Now turn down the heat a little, and add another ½ tablespoon of oil to the wok. When the oil is hot, add the spring onion, which will make a good percussive sound; as soon as this sound has faded, put in all the prepared vegetables, together with 2 pinches of salt and 1 heaped dessertspoon of sugar. Mix together. Then add the following, one by one, to develop a sauce-like texture: 2 dessertspoons of light soy sauce, 3 tablespoons of hot water from the kettle, 1 teaspoon of Chinese white rice vinegar, 1 teaspoon of Chinese cooking rice wine, and ⅓ dessertspoon of cornflour already mixed with a little water (enough to cover it in a small bowl). Now turn the heat up higher and mix; the ingredients should be bubbling in the wok. Finally, add a drizzle of sesame seed oil, and pour the contents of your wok over the fish, as though covering it with a colourful blanket. This part of the cooking process should take about 3–4 minutes.

Serve the fish with steamed rice, perhaps a dish of potato with Sichuan pepper, and another of celery or beansprouts with egg.

Chilli option: if you would like to include chilli in this dish, when you fry the spring onion, do so with two finely chopped fresh chillies (one red, one green) until they shrink and begin to change colour. Only then do you add the other prepared vegetables and the ingredients to make the sauce.

Prawns and (Green Flower) Broccoli

I couldn't buy broccoli – the Chinese say 'green flowers' – in my childhood, but it is a vegetable that goes beautifully with seafood. This dish demonstrates the beauty of simplicity in Chinese cooking, which depends on accurate timing and an emphasis on the natural qualities of individual ingredients; the deep, fresh greenness and crunchy texture of the broccoli combine brilliantly with the pale pink, chewy prawns, their distinctive smell of the sea emanating from the dish.

INGREDIENTS

1 broccoli head, about 400 g (14 oz), torn by hand into little florets
sunflower oil
1 spring onion, washed, divided in half lengthwise and finely chopped
10–15 tiger prawns, peeled and deheaded
1½ teaspoons Chinese cooking rice wine
sesame seed oil
sea salt

METHOD

First, bring some water to the boil and add the broccoli florets, cooking them for 3 minutes only before draining through a colander. Heat your wok until it is warm and add 1½ tablespoons of sunflower oil. Continue to heat until the oil is hot, almost smoking, and then add the spring onion, creating a percussive sound. After about 5 seconds, when the sound has quietened and the spring onion has curled, add the prawns. Stir them with a wooden spoon for 2–3 minutes until they turn a reddish colour. Now add the broccoli florets and toss, or move around in the wok with a wooden spoon. Finally, add the cooking wine, a drizzle of sesame seed oil and a few pinches of salt to taste. Give a final toss, combining all the ingredients, to ensure that the broccoli absorbs all the natural flavours while retaining its distinctive texture and emerald-green colour.

Trout with Coriander

One of the modern recipes I am including for you. This is a very fresh, natural dish in which the green coriander contrasts with the white fish, and every ingredient can be tasted individually. The fish is extremely light, delicate and tender – and my children love it!

INGREDIENTS

4 spring onions – cut off the green sections, and put to one side; divide the onions in half lengthwise, and continue dividing them until you have very thin strips; slice these diagonally; then prepare the green parts of the onions in exactly the same way

5 slices of ginger from a medium bulb, peeled and cut into very thin strips

3 cloves of garlic, crushed and finely chopped

2 teaspoons white caster sugar

1 tablespoon Western red or white wine vinegar

1½ tablespoons light soy sauce

½ tablespoon Chinese cooking rice wine

1 whole trout, about 400–450 g (14 oz–1 lb), or 2 small trout weighing the equivalent

A handful of fresh coriander, finely chopped

2½ tablespoons sunflower oil

1 fresh, small red chilli pepper (optional), chopped lengthwise into fine strips, following the shape of the chilli

a few drops of sesame seed oil

METHOD

First, put the water on to boil, and then prepare all the ingredients as described above. Place the spring onion, ginger, garlic and sugar in a bowl, and then spoon on the vinegar, soy sauce and rice wine. Mix well.

When the water is boiling, put in the fish so that it is completely covered, and turn down the heat to prevent overboiling. Allow to boil for 7 minutes, until the trout is tender. Take the fish out carefully and place it in a long dish. Pour on the mixture so that it completely coats the trout. Heap the fresh coriander on to the top.

Now prepare the sunflower oil; it is essential to get this right. First, heat your wok until it is warm, and then add the oil. Turn the heat up high for a few minutes, until the oil is smoking – at this point it is extremely hot, so be careful! But also, don't be too timid, because if the oil isn't hot enough the dish won't work at all. At this point, once the oil is smoking, add the chilli (this is optional) and, after a few seconds, carefully pour the oil all over the fish. It should make a dramatic, crackling sound as the tastes of all the different ingredients are absorbed and combined. This sound means your dish is very successful! Do this in the kitchen, near the wok, as it will spit.

Finally, add a few drops of sesame seed oil, and the trout is ready to be taken to the table. Serve accompanied by steamed rice.

Other fish that can be cooked in this way are sea bass and salmon, preferably organic, weighing about 400–450 g (14 oz–1 lb).

SOUPS

In China soup is traditionally served at the end of a meal, to fill in the little spaces as though completing a wall. Follow with some fresh fruit and perhaps sunflower seeds. We find this far more refreshing and healthy than serving sweet things; though my sisters can never resist a piece of chocolate!

Winter Melon, Glass Noodles and Meatball Soup

If you go to a specialist Chinese food shop, you should be able to find *dong gua* (winter melon), a dark-emerald-green vegetable, similar in shape and size to its relation the watermelon. Combined in this clear, tasty soup with pork and ginger meatballs and transparent glass noodles, it is beautifully refreshing after all the tastes and colours of the preceding dishes. When I was little, I used to love seeing the pattern emerging on the bottom of the bowl as I finished my soup.

INGREDIENTS

winter melon, usually sold in big slices, about 5 cm (2 in) thick –
    use half of one large slice
1 dessertspoon very finely chopped ginger
2 spring onions, washed and finely chopped (both green and
    white parts)
150 g (5½ oz) organic or free-range minced pork
sea salt
1 egg white
cornflour

ingredients continue ➤

1¼ litres (2 pints) meat stock – traditionally you would make
    your own, using pork and chicken bones; if you buy your
    stock, make sure it is as natural as possible
1 packet of *fen-si* (green-bean thread noodles, also known as
    glass noodles) – remove the string, and then cut one handful
    (quite a tricky manoeuvre!)
a few thick slices of ginger
sesame seed oil
a little finely chopped fresh coriander (optional)

METHOD

Begin by preparing the winter melon: remove the seeds and
the tough skin. Cut the flesh into large pieces and then into
the palest green, rectangular slices – but not paper-thin. Put
to one side.

Then, to make the meatballs, in a bowl add the chopped
ginger and one of the finely chopped spring onions to the
minced pork, with a few pinches of sea salt, followed by the
egg white and two heaped teaspoons of cornflour, mixing all
the ingredients together very thoroughly. The egg white
makes the meatballs tender, the cornflour keeps their shape.

In a medium-size pan bring the meat stock to the boil, and
add a little sea salt. Using a teaspoon, form your pork mixture
into little balls and put them into the stock to cook for a
couple of minutes. Then put in the glass noodles and winter
melon slices, together with a few thick slices of ginger. Continue to boil for a further 4 minutes, until the melon has
become soft and transparent, like the glass noodles. Sprinkle
some of the remaining chopped spring onion on to the
surface of the soup, and drizzle a little sesame seed oil over the
top. Finally, if you like, add a sprinkling of fresh, finely
chopped coriander.

Huang-gua xi-hong-shi

CUCUMBER AND TOMATO SOUP

This is the soup that arrived by bicycle after our performance in Tiananmen Square. Refreshing and warming at the same time, it has colours that I love: red and green, with yellow clouds of egg. In the *hutong*s it is called *qing tang* (pure soup).

INGREDIENTS

½ cucumber, unpeeled
1 large tomato, unpeeled
4 slices of unpeeled ginger
sea salt
1 egg, well beaten with chopsticks
1 spring onion, finely chopped
sesame seed oil
a handful of fresh coriander, finely chopped (optional)

METHOD

Cut the cucumber in half lengthwise, then slice very finely into semicircles and put into a dish. Cut the tomato in half and then slice it into crescent-moon shapes, about 12 segments in all. Put 1 litre (2 pints) of water into a medium saucepan, add the slices of ginger and bring to the boil, adding ½ teaspoon of salt. Now add the tomato and cucumber, keeping the heat on high. After 2–3 minutes, you are ready to add the clouds of egg, using a special technique: putting your two chopsticks to the far lip of the bowl containing the beaten egg, drizzle the egg slowly through and over the chopsticks, creating pale gold-yellow clouds. Turn off the heat immediately, and add the spring onion, followed by a long drizzle of sesame seed oil. Serve, topped with a sprinkling of fresh coriander if you wish.

DUMPLINGS

These are the most symbolic, and for me the most evocative examples of Chinese home cooking. There are many different kinds of traditional parcels, made with white wheat-flour, and filled with a combination of vegetables, meat, fish and seafood: *baozi* (made with self-raising flour, and folded to look like flowers when steamed); *herzi* (shaped like secret boxes), spring rolls, of course, but the most famous, ancient and pleasurable of them all, for anyone who has grown up in the Beijing alleys, are the symbolic *jiaozi* (boiled dumplings) and *hun-tun* (little dumpling) soup.

Hun-tun tang

LITTLE DUMPLING SOUP

Hun-tun is a traditional soup combining a nutritious stock with handmade flour parcels containing pork and ginger. It remained a favourite of my mother's throughout her life. Traditionally it was eaten late in the evening, after going to the theatre.

In this recipe I have added tiger prawns, which combine beautifully with the pork and ginger to give an even more delicious taste.

INGREDIENTS

For the stock

If you are making your own stock, you will need to collect leftovers from other dishes – such as prawn shells, chicken bones, fish skin, spare ribs – which you must boil and then simmer with a little sea salt for many hours in a large pan. It is worth the effort, because

236

you will create a beautiful, natural, nutritious base for your soup. Of course, you can use a ready-made stock, but make sure the ingredients are as natural as possible.

For the dumplings and to serve

170 g (6 oz) plain flour
90 ml (3 fl oz) cold water
110 g (4 oz) organic or free-range minced pork
15 tiger prawns, peeled and deheaded
1 spring onion, finely chopped
1 small piece of ginger, finely chopped
light soy sauce
sea salt
Chinese cooking rice wine (I recommend Shaoxing rice wine)
1 egg, beaten
sesame seed oil
a handful of fresh coriander, finely chopped

METHOD

To make the dough: first put the flour into a bowl and make a well in the centre. Then begin to drizzle the cold water into the well, a little at a time, stirring with chopsticks around the edge of the well to incorporate the flour and form little lumps. Continue to drizzle the water wherever the flour is still dry, stirring until the dough begins to form. Then begin kneading with your hands, until you have a piece of dough like a round, very smooth stone, medium-soft. Leave this to rest for 20–30 minutes.

Rolling the dough: take a piece of your dough, about the size of a mini bread roll, and knead it again, turning and folding it. Then, using a wooden rolling pin, roll your dough as thin as paper, into a round shape. Cut into strips, then into triangles. We call these triangles the *hun-tun pi* (dumpling skins). You need to think in terms of making 6–10 little dumplings for each person, so make as many as you need. (You can, of course, buy these skins ready-made in a Chinese food shop, but making your own is really worth the additional time and effort.)

To make the stuffing: chop the minced pork and prawns very, very finely (we say they are 'mashed') and mix with the spring onion and ginger. Add a little light soy sauce, a few pinches of sea salt, a few drops of Chinese cooking rice wine and one beaten egg. Mix well.

To make the *hun-tun*: taking a little of your stuffing mixture, place it towards one corner of a triangle and fold that corner over, to cover the mixture. Then fold again in the same direction, so that you can't see the mixture except through the ends of this little roll. Then, holding your thumbs a third of the way along from either end, twist and turn up, joining the two remaining corners. It's a beautiful action.

Cooking the *hun-tun*: take some of the stock from your large pan, and bring to the boil in a saucepan. Put the *hun-tun* into the boiling stock for about 3-4 minutes to cook.

To serve: taking some blue and white porcelain bowls and spoons, put into each bowl a little finely chopped spring onion, 2-3 drops of sesame seed oil and a drizzle of light soy sauce. Then ladle the *hun-tun* parcels and soup into each bowl, giving 6-10 little dumplings to each person. As a final touch, sprinkle on some finely chopped fresh coriander.

Jiaozi

TRADITIONAL BEIJING DUMPLINGS

The traditional filling for home-made *jiaozi* in the Beijing alleys is pork, *bai-cai* (Chinese leaf) and ginger, but the beauty of these dumplings is that the creative possibilities are almost endless! I love now to use fish and prawns with cabbage, *bai-*

cai or marrow; another delicious possibility is French beans with pork; and I have also created 'woodland *jiaozi*', using dried lily-flower, wood-ear and bamboo as ingredients for the stuffing. Other options include lamb or beef with *bai-cai*: very tasty, but much heavier than the pork or seafood versions.

A few important points to remember: you must squeeze your Chinese leaf thoroughly after you have chopped it very finely and sprinkled it with salt, as described below, otherwise your filling will be too wet and the dumplings will fall apart during cooking; you must chop your ingredients very evenly and finely, the secret to good *jiaozi*; and you must take time to enjoy the whole process of making them, preferably with family or friends.

Jiaozi with Pork, Prawns, Bai-Cai and Ginger

The prawns are a modern, very tasty addition to this recipe from the *hutongs*. I learned to make *jiaozi* the traditional way, by sight and feel, never by measuring quantities. For example, making the dough has for me always been about balancing the flour and water by hand until just the right texture is achieved; of course, this takes practice and experience. We would also use simply as much or as little pork as we had, adjusting the other ingredients accordingly; and fresh eggs were not always available. So I would say that making traditional *jiaozi* is not so much about following strict rules regarding the ingredients, but more about using your imagination, feeling and experience. Each person has his or her own individual touch. Of course, this is a complex recipe to follow for the first time on paper, but the actions involved lie at the very heart of home cooking in the alleys. Ideally, try to attend a workshop, to follow and learn the actions at first hand; you can then practise at home. In my childhood, the time and effort involved were expressions of love, and for me the art of making dumplings is still about this.

INGREDIENTS (FOR 100 DUMPLINGS)

670 g (1½ lb) plain white flour
330 ml (11 fl oz) cold water
1 *bai-cai* (Chinese leaf), very finely chopped, sprinkled with sea salt, and left for 20 minutes before being squeezed through muslin to remove all water
225 g (8 oz) extra-lean minced pork, free-range or organic
10–12 tiger prawns, peeled, deheaded and very finely chopped (we say 'mashed') (optional ingredient)
4 spring onions, very finely chopped (use both white and green parts)
ginger, 15 g (½ oz) piece, peeled and finely chopped
sunflower oil
2 eggs, beaten
dark soy sauce
Chinese cooking rice wine
sea salt
sesame seed oil

For the traditional garlic sauce

5 cloves of garlic, peeled and finely chopped
Chinese dark rice vinegar (I use Chinkiang vinegar, which tastes a bit like Italian balsamic vinegar)
sesame seed oil

For my own special sauce

The same ingredients as for the above sauce with, in addition, brown sugar, soy sauce and chilli oil (optional)

METHOD

To make the dough: put the flour into a large bowl, and begin to drizzle cold water on to it, a little at a time, moving the flour around with a pair of chopsticks as it starts to form lumps and pieces. Continue to drizzle the water only on to the remaining dry flour until there is no more to be seen; then begin using your hands to form and knead the evolving dough. Continue kneading until you have made a large, rounded dough, like a smooth, sensual stone, not too soft. Leave it to rest for about 30 minutes while you prepare your stuffing.

To make the stuffing: ensure that the *bai-cai* is very finely chopped and thoroughly squeezed (through a piece of muslin), then put it into a bowl. Add to this your prepared pork, prawns, spring onion and ginger. Heat your wok, add 2½ tablespoons of oil, wait until the oil is just smoking and then add the two beaten eggs, moving them around briskly in all directions over the high heat until the pieces are golden and crispy; add these to the dish. Then add the following: 2 tablespoons of light soy sauce, 7 tablespoons of sunflower oil, ¾ tablespoon of cooking rice wine, three good pinches of sea salt (adjust to suit your taste) and a drizzle or teaspoon of sesame seed oil. Your stuffing is now prepared.

Making the dough circles: take one handful of dough, form it with your hands into a long sausage shape, about 2½ cm (1 in) in diameter, and cut into small pieces, about 2½ cm (1 in) long. Taking each piece, form into a ball shape and then flatten with the palm of your hand, creating a disc about 3½ cm (1¼–1½ in) in diameter. Then, using a rolling pin (we use a small one for this), roll the dough into a circle, turning it as you roll to form a circular dumpling skin, about 7–8 cm (3 in) in diameter, with a thicker centre to hold the weight of the stuffing. Make 100 of these! Of course, you can buy them ready-made in a specialist Chinese food shop, but nothing compares to the home-made ones.

Making the *jiaozi* (dumplings): for each dumpling, put 1½ teaspoons of stuffing into the centre of a dough circle, bring the top and bottom edges together and press with your fingers to seal the dough. You now have a half-moon shape, with the filling concealed, but the ends open. You are now going to seal first one, then the other end. Holding the dumpling in your left hand (if you are right handed), push the bottom of the open end up to the top, using your right index finger, thereby creating two loops. Seal the loop that is closer to you by pressing the two edges together with your thumb and forefinger. Then press the top of the other loop as though creating two further loops (like two ears) and flatten against the dumpling, pressing the edges together with your thumb and first finger so that you create two folds, which are visible if you look at the back of your dumpling. Now change hands and seal the other end in the same way. There should be four folds on the back of each dumpling. This is the traditional folding technique, which has been used for thousands of years. In the alleys, dumplings are arranged on big circular straw mats in a very orderly fashion, prior to cooking. Please note: If you find this traditional folding technique difficult to master the first time, seal the corners by creating little concertina-like folds as you press the edges together: it is crucial that they do not open during the cooking process.

To make *suan zhi* (garlic sauce), the traditional sauce for dumplings: finely chop 5 peeled cloves of garlic. Then put 4 dessertspoons of Chinese dark rice vinegar into a bowl, with a drizzle of sesame seed oil. Traditionally you would now add the garlic; this is your sauce.

To make my own special sauce: in addition to the 4 dessert-spoons of vinegar, I like to add 1 teaspoon of brown sugar, 1 tablespoon of very good soy sauce and a drizzle of sesame seed oil. Add the garlic if you like, and ½ teaspoon of chilli oil, also if you like (in Chinese homes they make their own). I find this sauce, with its touch of sweetness, goes beautifully with the pork and prawn stuffing.

Cooking the *jiaozi*: put a large, deep saucepan of water on to boil. When the water is boiling, put in around 20 dumplings at a time – very carefully because they break easily. As the dumplings go into the water, they sink down because they are heavy and the water goes 'dead'. Now use a wooden spoon to stir the water – not the dumplings – round in one direction, spinning the water to create a kind of whirlpool which allows the dumplings to float and move in the water. When the dumplings are 'up' and floating, put the lid on the pan and wait for 2 minutes. Be careful not to let the water boil over, so stay with your dumplings. When the water is really boiling again, remove the lid and add a few drops of cold water, then leave the lid off for a couple of minutes. The water will boil again. When it does so, add a few more drops of cold water and wait once more. It will boil for a third time. Then add a few more drops of cold water. The dumplings are now ready to come out of the water; remove them using a draining spoon and serve on a flat plate, accompanied by a bowl of sauce.

Jiaozi can also be fried, but at home the Chinese prefer these lighter, healthier dumplings.

To eat: put a dessertspoon of sauce into your bowl, and pick up a dumpling with your chopsticks – quite a challenge if you are a novice! The *jiaozi* will be very hot, so bite the end of your first one to let out the steam. In China we have an old saying: 'If you are a person with a "hurrying heart", without patience, then you cannot eat beautiful dumplings – you will burn yourself!' It is really a pleasure to see friends and family enjoying dumplings together, with flushed faces and laughter. Children love to keep count of how many they have eaten.

NOODLES

Handmade Flour Noodles

Noodles are eaten throughout China, and are highly symbolic: they represent long life and are considered to be very good for your health. Made from wheat flour, eggs and water, we call them *mian-tiao* (flour ribbons). There are many different methods of making noodles, and each part of China has its own regional style. Mine are typical home-made noodles, similar to those made by the singers from the countryside in my father's Dancing and Singing Ensemble.

INGREDIENTS

280 g (10 oz) plain flour, in a big bowl
1 egg
half a glass of warm water

METHOD

Break the egg into the flour and mix with your fingers. Drip the water slowly into the mixture, gathering it up into your fingers until it forms moist lumps – don't allow it to get wet. Then start kneading the mixture into a dough. As you knead, the mixture will become a whole lump of dough; it should be quite hard. If you are a good noodle-maker, you will make sure at this point that your hands, the bowl – everything – is clean and shining. If you are neat, and you don't leave flour everywhere, you will make good noodles! Now lay a piece of wet muslin over the dough and leave it to rest for about 20 minutes.

Find a big work surface and spread a lot of flour on to it, using circular hand-movements. Using a large rolling pin, begin to roll your dough: this bit is hard work. As you roll, turn the dough over, apply more flour, and roll again. Keep rolling and turning, until your dough is a thin round sheet. Now wrap the dough around your rolling pin, using a lot of flour, and roll again to make the dough even thinner. When it is round and as thin as a wine glass, it is ready to be made into noodles.

Roll nearly all the dough around your rolling pin, so that only a little is left on the work surface. Then begin to fold it like a concertina, moving the pin first one way and then another, putting flour between each folded layer, each fold being about 5 cm (2 in) wide. The middle of this pile of folds will be thicker than the ends because of the circular shape of the dough. Now, using a sharp knife, cut the dough in half down the middle, and then slice each half into roughly equal strips - narrow, medium or wide, depending on the shape you wish your noodles to be. Now you can unravel them.

These are your handmade noodles.

Tang mian

NOODLE SOUP WITH TOMATO AND CARROT

My earliest memory of noodles is of a very simple bowl of noodle soup. We would eat this in the winter, when it is very, very cold in the north of China. There are maybe one hundred different kinds of *tang mian*, made with lamb, beef, pork, seafood or just pure vegetables; this last we say is for the monks. When I was little we would have just a few vegetables in our noodle soup, because meat was too expensive. I remember tomatoes with spring onion and finely sliced ginger: this would heat your body, making you really warm. By contrast, in the hot summers we would eat iced noodles: peanuts were ground into a paste, with salt and very thinly sliced cucumber, and this mixture would be added to the cold noodles, making a well-known dish.

In this recipe, you can use dried noodles or fresh, hand-made noodles; just remember to adjust the cooking time.

INGREDIENTS

sunflower oil
1 spring onion, washed and finely chopped
light soy sauce
1¼ litres (2 pints) hot water from the kettle
1 carrot, sliced finely into pieces 3 cm (1¼ in) long – first cut the carrot in half crosswise, then again lengthwise, so that you have four pieces to slice thinly, at a slight angle, to make interesting shapes
2 tomatoes (we say *xi-hong*, meaning 'west red'), cut into small segments, with the skin still on
sea salt
noodles, good wheat-flour or handmade
1 egg (optional)
sesame seed oil

METHOD

Heat your wok until it is hot, and then add 2 tablespoons of sunflower oil. When the oil is very hot, put in most of the spring onion, which should make a gentle percussive sound. When this has died down, and the spring onion has begun to shrink, add 1½ tablespoons of light soy sauce. Leave for about 10 seconds and then add 1¼ litres (2 pints) of hot water from the kettle. Place a lid on the wok and bring to the boil.

When the water is boiling, add the carrots and tomatoes, together with 2–3 pinches of salt, before adding the noodles. If you are using handmade noodles, they will take less time to cook than dried ones (2–3 minutes, compared with 4–5 minutes for dried noodles). First, lift them up and dance with them a little, to shake off the loose flour. When the vegetables have been cooking for about 6 minutes, put in 2 or 3 handfuls of the noodles, loosening and evenly distributing them as you put them into the water. Don't touch them for 20 seconds. Then, using your chopsticks, start to move them around gently. After about a minute you can, if you like, break an egg into the soup, and leave it to cook; this makes the soup more nutritious. When the soup is ready, add a drizzle of sesame seed oil and the remaining spring onion, and serve.

Whenever we were ill as children, my mother would always want us to have noodle soup, as well as pickles!

Seafood Tang Mian (Noodle Soup) with Scallops, Prawns, Squid and Handmade Noodles

In China, noodle styles differ enormously between the north and the south. In the north we like strong tastes, with salt, soy sauce, lots of vegetables, meat. In the south, very light, pure noodles are eaten. In Shanghai, for example, there is a famous white noodle soup containing only a little spring onion, white noodles and a drop of sesame seed oil. It is called *yang chun mian* (weeping willow spring noodles) – very pure, very simple. In Shanghai they think this is incredible for your body. Of course, the key to this *tang mian* lies in the actual soup: a stock is used, made from chicken bones, spare ribs and prawn shells, boiled for many hours. So this white noodle soup actually has a very beautiful, deep taste.

The recipe that follows is for a modern seafood *tang mian*, which is now my favourite. Unlike egg and tomato soup, or winter melon soup, it is not served at the end of a meal, but forms the main part of the meal, to be followed perhaps by a couple of tasty dishes such as shredded pork with pickles, diced pork with red and green pepper, or organic celery with crispy egg.

INGREDIENTS

material for the stock – a chicken leg, prawn shells, sliced ginger and spring onion, and sea salt (you could of course use a ready-made stock instead, ideally one containing only natural ingredients)
handmade or dried noodles (remember that dried noodles will take longer to boil)
fresh scallops, tiger prawns (peeled and deheaded) and thinly sliced squid
sesame seed oil
light soy sauce
2 spring onions, washed and finely chopped
a handful of fresh coriander, finely chopped

METHOD

Two hours or more before you begin cooking the noodles, make the stock: add your stock material to a pan of boiling water, and leave to simmer for at least 2 hours – the longer the better. Once drained, this is your stock for the soup.

When your stock is ready, bring a pan of water to boil for the noodles. Handmade noodles have a lot of excess flour, so lift them up and dance with them first, to shake off the loose flour. When the water is boiling, put in 2 or 3 handfuls of noodles, loosening and evenly distributing them as you put them into the water. Don't touch them for 20 seconds. Then, using your chopsticks, start to move them around gently. After a couple of minutes, drain the noodles and keep to one side.

Now, judging how much liquid will be just enough for the soup, pour your stock into the empty pan, and add the prepared seafood; leave for 2-3 minutes to boil. The prawns will redden, the squid will curl into shape.

Finally, using chopsticks, transfer one serving of noodles to a big, beautiful bowl for each person and then, using a ladle, pour some soup and seafood over the noodles. Drizzle a little sesame seed oil and very good soy sauce on to the soup and sprinkle on some of the finely chopped spring onion and coriander. The soup is now ready to serve.

INDEX

Note: page numbers in **bold** refer to photographs and illustrations.

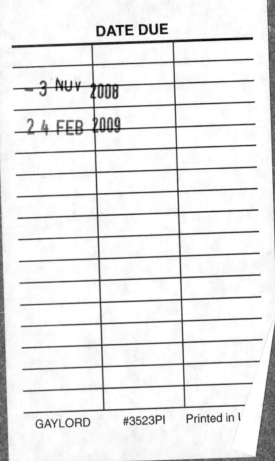